The Millennium Project

STATE OF THE

FUTURE

V. 19.0

**Jerome C. Glenn, Elizabeth Florescu,
and The Millennium Project Team**

RECOMMENDATIONS

An important example of using scientific methods and collective intelligence to help us understand and act better for the future.
> Phil Mjwara, Director General, Ministry of Science & Technology, South Africa

Outstanding report!
> Jim Spohrer, Director, Cognitive Opentech Group, IBM

A high level, reliable intellectual compass for the conflict ridden, and uncertain world advancing toward the mid-century.
> Mihály Simai, former Chairman, United Nations University

One of the best studies of modern terrorism and what to do about it.
> Jamie Shea, Deputy Asst. Secretary General, NATO

Strategic planning for the planet; must reading for world leaders.
> William Halal, President, TechCast Global

The indispensable guide for futurists and aspiring global citizens everywhere
> Hazel Henderson, Futurist, author, CEO, Ethical Markets Media

Without this kind of guidance, many people would lose their way and get lost in their decision making process.
> Julio Millan, President, Azteca Corporation, Mexico

*The **State of the Future** has proved useful for better addressing our resilience objectives.*
> Lina Liakou, Thessaloniki Vice Mayor and Chief Resilience Officer

Great source of inspiration and focus to our organizations.
> Michael Bodekaer, CEO, Learn-Technologies

*The **State of the Future** gives invaluable insights into the future.*
> Ban Ki-moon, former Secretary-General, United Nations

ISBN: 978-0-9882639-5-6   Library of Congress Control No: 98-646672

© 2017 The Millennium Project
4421 Garrison Street, NW   +1-202-686-5179 (F/P)
Washington, D.C. 20016-4055 U.S.A.   info@millennium-project.org

The *State of the Future* is a publication of The Millennium Project, an international participatory think tank established in 1996.

TABLE OF CONTENTS

ACKNOWLEDGMENTS

The Chairs and Co-chairs of the 63 Millennium Project Nodes, plus their members who help select participants for studies and national workshops, translate questionnaires, scenarios, and studies, initiate projects, review text, and conduct interviews, are essential for the success of the research and entire work of The Millennium Project. Their unique contributions to this and previous years' *State of the Future* reports are greatly appreciated.

Jerome Glenn and Elizabeth Florescu were partners in the research and production of this volume. Jerome Glenn wrote the executive summary, provided the leadership on the cumulative research on the 15 Global Challenges in Chapter 1, conducted the three Real-Time Delphis on each of the Future Work/Technology 2050 Global Scenarios, wrote the initial and final drafts of these scenarios in Chapter 4, and oversaw the national workshops and their suggestions listed in Chapter 4. Elizabeth Florescu and Theodore Gordon computed the 2015 State of the Future Index in Chapter 2. Elizabeth Florescu managed the NATO Advanced Research Workshop on Emerging Technologies and New Counter-Terror Strategies and produced the final synthesis in Chapter 3 with inputs from Theodore Gordon, Yair Sharon, and Jerome Glenn.

The reviewers of the initial drafts of the 15 Global Challenges included Amara Angelica, Gregory Brown, Dennis Bushnell, Puruesh Chaudhary, Henry Cole, Jose Cordeiro, Cornelia Daheim, Tony Diggle, Elizabeth Florescu, Greg Folkers, Paula Gordon, Theodore Gordon, Odette Gregory, William Halal, Sirkka Heinonen, Mary Herman, James Hochschwender, Philip Horvath, Candice Hughes, Ted Kahn, Nikolaos Kastrinos, Steve Killelea, Hayato Kobayashi, Gerd Leonhard, Mark Lupisella, John Mankins, Mario Marais, Michael McDonald, Eszter Monda, Thomas Murphy, Concepción Olavarrieta, Charles Ostman, Gordian Raacke, Diann Rodgers-Healey, Sheila Ronis, Paulo Rossetti, Yashar Saghai, Geci Karuri Sebina, Linda Thornton, Sesh Velamoor, Pera Wells, and Axel Zweck.

The Millennium Project Interns who conducted research for this report and the Global Futures Intelligence System that updates this report were Zahra Asghar, Elaine Cavalheiro, Antoniya Dineva, Hazel Hadian, Clairisse Haines, Chaebin Han, Seokryu Hong, Yifan Hu, Marit Hunt, Niccolò Invidia, Luxing Jiang, Matthew Jones, Xiongxiong Kang, Shreyak Khanal, Jimin Kim, Jude Herijadi Kurniawan, Gema León, Zirui Liao, Jane Nakasamu, Sânziana Onac, Brenda Ongola-Jacob, Verónica Parra, Dheeya Rizmie, Nicholas Ryu, Shyama Sadashiv, Sida Shu, Suraj Sood, Nadja Wipp, Louay Youssef, and Sunny Zhang.

Special thanks to Wesley Boyer for trouble-shooting the Global Futures Intelligence System at themp.org that was used extensively to produce this report. Updating the 15 Global Challenges of the ***State of the Future*** is an ongoing process in the GFIS, which also has weblinks to references for much of the data that are not visible in this print edition.

Linda Starke provided editing and proofreading. Elizabeth Florescu did the production and layout of this publication.

And special gratitude for donations from readers like you, who help our work continue. Contributions to The Millennium Project are tax-deductible for taxpayers in the United States, as it is a 501(c)(3) nonprofit organization.

PREFACE

Today's information overloaded world needs coherence, frameworks, and context to get a sense of the big picture of how we are doing and foreseeable prospects. Taken together, the very short overviews of the 15 Global Challenges offer a systemic framework for understanding global change.

A complete description of the global situation, prospects for the future, and strategies to achieve the best possible future is—of course—impossible, but enough is presented in the *State of the Future* to improve the readers' global foresight. Far greater information and intelligence is available in the Global Futures Intelligence System at www.themp.org, where the subscriber can also participate in updating and improving this collective intelligence system on the future of the world.

The *State of the Future Version 19.0* brings together an extraordinarily diverse set of data, information, intelligence, and, we hope, some wisdom about the future. This is the nineteenth edition of the *State of the Future*. We believe that each edition is better than the previous one. We update data, improve insights, and respond to feedback. Over the years, the short overviews in each *State of the Future* report kept getting longer, and they became too long to say they are "short." In this edition, they are shorter. We hope you like them. The longer "Short Overviews" with regional considerations will still be available free online and updated regularly in the GFIS, which is also available on your mobile phone, for just-in-time information.

Since humanity lives in different conditions around the world, not all of the actions suggested to address the Global Challenges are appropriate in all situations; think of them as a menu of options and a source of stimulation to develop more appropriate strategies to your unique situation. The suggested actions are drawn from feedback on previous *State of the Future* reports, Millennium Project Delphi studies, and GFIS's news feeds, scanning items, situation updates, and peer reviewers' comments.

This is the third time we have used the online GFIS to update and improve the *State of the Future* report. The challenges in GFIS are updated regularly from news aggregations, scanning items, situation charts, and other resources, which has led to greater detail and depth than in the previous edition. While this report presents the distilled results of recent research by The Millennium Project, GFIS contains the detailed background and data for that research, plus all of The Millennium Project's research since its founding in 1996. It also contains the largest internationally peer-reviewed set of methods to explore future possibilities ever assembled in one source. Readers of this report are encouraged to subscribe to GFIS to keep up to date and to participate in improving insights about future possibilities.

Following is a screenshot of the GFIS homepage:

The purpose of futures research is to systematically explore, create, and test both possible and desirable futures in order to improve decisions. Just as the person on top of the mast on old sailing ships used to point out the rocks and safe channels to the captain below for the smooth running of the ship through uncharted waters, so too can futurists with foresight systems point out problems and opportunities to leaders and the public around the world.

Since decisionmaking is increasingly affected by globalization, global futures research is increasingly needed for decisionmaking by individuals, groups, and institutions. The quality of democracies emerging around the world depends on the quality of information received by the public. The issues and opportunities addressed in this report can contribute to better-informed decisionmaking.

This report is for thought leaders, decisionmakers, and all those who care about the world and its future. Readers will learn how their interests fit into the global situation and how the global situation may affect them and their interests. The *State of the Future* and GFIS provide an additional eye on global change. These are information utilities that you can draw from as relevant to your unique needs. They provide an overview of the global strategic landscape. Business executives use the research as input to their strategic planning. University professors, futurists, and other consultants find this information useful in teaching and research.

The Millennium Project is a voluntary global participatory think tank of futurists, scholars, scientists, business planners, and policymakers who work for international organizations, governments, corporations, NGOs, and universities and who volunteer their time to improve each edition of the *State of the Future*. It was selected to be among the top think tanks in the world for new ideas and paradigms as well as for best quality assurance and integrity policies and procedures by the 2013-2016 University of Pennsylvania's GoTo Think Tank Index and as a 2012 Computerworld Honors Laureate for its innovations in collective intelligence systems.

The purposes of The Millennium Project are to assist in organizing futures research, improve thinking about the future, and make that thinking available through a variety of media for consideration in policymaking, advanced training, public education, and feedback, ideally in order to accumulate wisdom about potential futures. The Project's diversity of opinions and global views is ensured by its 63 Nodes around the world. These are groups of individuals and organizations that interconnect global and local perspectives. They identify participants, conduct interviews, translate and distribute questionnaires, and conduct research and conferences. It is through their contributions that the world picture of this report and indeed all of The Millennium Project's work emerges. The Node Chairs and Co-chairs are listed in the Appendix.

Through its research, publications, addresses at conferences, and Nodes, The Millennium Project helps to nurture an international collaborative spirit of free inquiry and feedback for increasing collective intelligence to improve social, technical, and environmental viability for human development. Feedback on any sections of the book is most welcome at <Jerome.Glenn@Millennium-Project.org> and may help shape the next *State of the Future*, GFIS, and the general work of The Millennium Project.

Jerome C. Glenn	Elizabeth Florescu	The Millennium Project Team
Executive Director	Director of Research	Staff, 63 Nodes, Reviewers,
The Millennium Project	The Millennium Project	and feedback from readers like you

EXECUTIVE SUMMARY

Most children born today are likely to be alive in the year 2100.

Imagine a world 50 years before then—2050—when the majority of the world could be augmented geniuses inventing their workday, every day, with new people, ideas, and experiences to make life worth living, and civilization could be far better than what we know today. However, without making good decisions, we can all imagine a future far worse than today. This *State of the Future 19.0* offers you data, information, intelligence, and some wisdom to provide a context or framework to help make better decisions than is commonly offered today.

Artificial intelligence will drive the development of quantum computing, and then quantum computing will further drive the development of artificial intelligence. This mutual acceleration could grow beyond human control and understanding. Scientific and technological leaders, advanced research institutes, and foundations are exploring how to anticipate and manage this issue.

Meanwhile, human life expectancy has increased from 46 years at birth in 1950 to 72 years now. Child mortality, poverty, contagious disease, and illiteracy have all decreased. The global nervous system of humanity is on the road to completion: 52% of the world—over 3.8 billion people—are now connected to the Internet, about two-thirds of the world has a mobile phone, and over half have smart phones. The Millennium Project's State of the

Future Index shows the world is expected to continue improving over the next 10 years (see Chapter 2); however, environmental conditions, armed conflicts, terrorism, and organized crime are getting worse.

The IMF expects growth of the world economy to increase from 3.1% percent in 2016 to 3.5% in 2017 and then 3.6 % in 2018. Given population growth at 1.11%, global income per capita is growing 2.39% annually.

Although extreme poverty fell from 51% in 1981 to 13% in 2012 and to less than 10% today, the concentration of wealth is increasing, income gaps are widening, jobless economic growth seems the new norm, and return on investment in capital and technology is usually better than labor. As labor costs go up and AI and robot costs go down, manufacturing and service unemployment rates will increase. Hence, new forms of economics seem inevitable if we are to avoid the social disasters of large-scale worldwide structural unemployment that have been forecast by many. Three alternative Future Work/Technology 2050 Global Scenarios in Chapter 4 show how different outcomes might evolve from these trends, along with 100 suggestions to address these issues from The Millennium Project national workshops held in 17 countries in 2016 and 2017. Other national workshops are being planned; taken together, they are intended to broaden and deepen the future of work conversation around the world, leading to improved long-range national policies.

The current world population of 7.6 billion is expected to grow another 2.2 billion in just 33 years (by 2050), putting pressure on food production, environmental management, and financial support systems. Although the world is aging, biological breakthroughs could dramatically extend the lives of healthy, mentally alert people way beyond what is believed today. Future migrations from low-income, high-youth-employment regions to high-income aging societies seem inevitable.

Eco-smart Cities are being built around the world, and older cities are being retrofitted with intelligent systems. China's One Belt, One Road initiative could lend up to $8 trillion for infrastructure in 68 countries to better connect China to Central Asia, the Middle East, and Europe, making it one of the greatest infrastructure projects in history, hopefully incorporating the latest eco-smart systems with AI. It may be that global urbanization is becoming too complex to manage without artificial intelligence. Moving workers to jobs creates massive traffic jams around the world. New technologies will make it increasingly easy to move jobs to workers. Recent calls for a "Fourth Industrial Revolution" that uses AI for all elements of production from market research to manufacturing and sales that are all connected in the cloud is expected to extend to everything from transportation and water management to power production and use.

Although over 90% of the world now has access to improved drinking water, water tables are falling on all continents, and nearly half of humanity gets its water from sources controlled by two or more countries. E-waste pollution is growing with poisonous effects on groundwater worldwide. As the developing world expands, its industries, agriculture, population growth, and GDP per capita income all rise and water consumption per capita will increase, making it impossible to avoid serious water crises and migrations unless major changes occur.

Increased atmospheric CO_2 that led to the Great Permian Extinction, killing 97% of life, could happen again if changes in food production, energy, and lifestyles do not occur. A trillion-ton chunk of ice twice the size of Luxembourg separated from the Antarctic ice shelf. The global cost of weather disasters increased from $94 billion in 2015 to $175 billion in 2016, according to SwissRe.

Although the vast majority of the world is living in peace and although armed conflicts fell dramatically from 1990 to 2010, conflicts have increased since then, and half the world is potentially unstable. The nature of warfare has morphed into transnational terrorism, international intervention into civil wars, as well as publicly denied cyber and information warfare. Information warfare (as distinct from cyber warfare that attacks computers, software, and command control systems) manipulates information trusted by targets without their awareness, so that the targets will make decisions against their interest but in the interest of the one conducting information warfare. Fake news via bots, videos, and other forms of information warfare are increasingly manipulating perceptions of truth, while the public does not know how to defend itself. Although the Internet has increased participation in governance and exposed corruption, press freedoms have decreased over the past several years, and anti-democratic forces are increasingly using new cyber tools to manipulate democratic processes.

Nuclear proliferation has not stopped, and future lone wolf terrorists may one day be able to make and deploy a weapon of mass destruction. Families and communities have to raise a new generation of more ethical people because government technical means and public mental health and education systems are not enough to guarantee a future free of the potential for individually active massively destructive technologies. Organized crime takes in over $3 trillion per year, which is twice that of all the military annual budgets combined. An estimated $1.5 trillion in bribes is paid per year; corruption is a major impediment to development for countries that are home to over 5 billion people. Distinctions among organized crime, corruption, insurgency, and terrorism have begun to blur, increasing threats to democracies, development, and security. A global strategy to counter this growth is needed in addition to the current nation-state, sectoral approaches.

Transnational and intercultural collaborations have reduced disease, created safer transportation systems around the world, and produced a global Internet that shares most of the world's knowledge at no or little coast. Neuroscience is showing how brain performance can be improved, and AI is being developed to figure out the best ways for you to learn and what you should, need to, and/or want to learn.

The percentage of women in parliaments, corporate boards, and other executive positions has increased slowly but steadily, although not fast enough to meet the UN Sustainable Development Goal to achieve gender equality and empower all women and girls by 2030. Some 50% of 10-year-olds live in countries with high levels of gender inequality.

The Paris Agreement is expected to reduce fossil fuel consumption and increase the use of renewable sources of energy. Coal use saw a dramatic reduction in 2016. Solar and wind energy are now cost-competitive with coal (especially when the cost of externalities are considered), and massive lithium-ion battery production plants are in construction to help renewables' ability to provide baseload electricity.

The speed of scientific breakthroughs and technological applications to improve the human condition is being accelerated by computational science and engineering, artificial intelligence, common database protocols, Moore's law, and Nielsen's law of Internet bandwidth (50% speed increase per year). Future synergies among synthetic biology, 3D/4D printing, artificial intelligence, robotics, atomically precise fabrication and other forms of nanotechnology, tele-everything, drones, augmented and virtual reality, falling costs of renewable energy systems, and collective intelligence systems will make the last 25 years of S&T change seem slow compared to the next 25.

Increasingly, decisions are being made by AI; since their algorithms are not ethically neutral, the future of ethics—in part—will be influenced by auditing ethical assumptions in software. Meanwhile, political spin masters drown out the pursuit of truth worldwide.

The moral will to act in collaboration across national, institutional, political, religious, and ideological boundaries that is necessary to address today's global challenges requires global ethics. Global ethics is emerging around the world through the evolution of ISO standards and international treaties that are defining the norms of civilization.

So, taken all together, how are we doing? Is the future in general getting better or worse?

To answer this, The Millennium Project with its Nodes around the world and the experts selected by Nodes have tracked progress and regress on 15 Global Challenges (see Chapter 1) for over 20 years and created a State of the Future Index (see Chapter 2).

The 2017 SOFI in Figure 1 shows that the world continues to improve in general, although at a slower pace than over the past 27 years. The rate of global improvement in SOFI for the coming decade will be 1.14%, versus 3.14% for the period 1990 to 2017. This is mostly due to the slow recovery after the 2008 financial crises and world recession in 2009. One of the variables that has a large impact on the 2017 SOFI projection is the number of terrorist attacks, which is very uncertain. If terrorism could be contained, the SOFI would appear considerably better. Chapter 3 provides experts' views from around the world on the future of terrorism and its deterrence.

Figure 1. State of the Future Index 2017

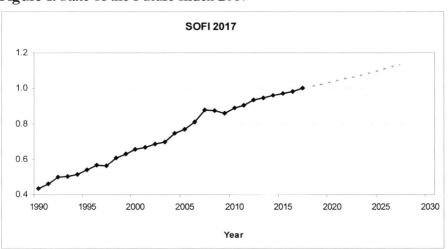

One of the advantages of computing the SOFI is the identification of the areas where we are winning, losing, or stagnating—thereby helping to set priorities. Figure 2 shows the trends of where humanity is winning and Figure 3 shows where we are losing or there is little progress. These are further analyzed in Chapter 2 by assessing the individual variables and their potential trajectories.

Figure 2. Where we are winning

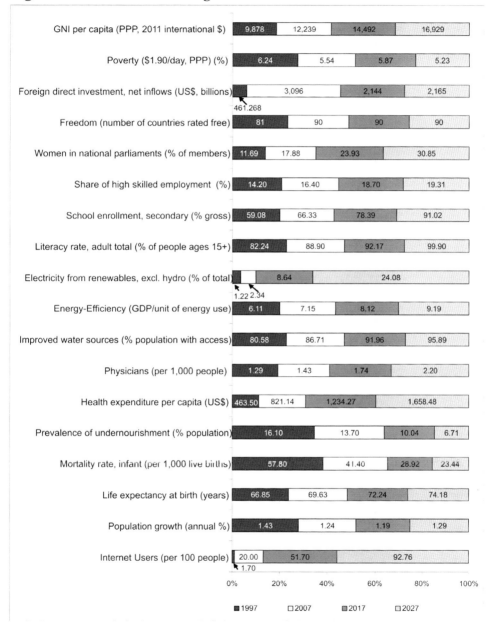

	1997	2007	2017	2027
GNI per capita (PPP, 2011 international $)	9,878	12,239	14,492	16,929
Poverty ($1.90/day, PPP) (%)	6.24	5.54	5.87	5.23
Foreign direct investment, net inflows (US$, billions)	461.268	3,096	2,144	2,165
Freedom (number of countries rated free)	81	90	90	90
Women in national parliaments (% of members)	11.69	17.88	23.93	30.85
Share of high skilled employment (%)	14.20	16.40	18.70	19.31
School enrollment, secondary (% gross)	59.08	66.33	78.39	91.02
Literacy rate, adult total (% of people ages 15+)	82.24	88.90	92.17	99.90
Electricity from renewables, excl. hydro (% of total)	1.22	2.34	8.64	24.08
Energy-Efficiency (GDP/unit of energy use)	6.11	7.15	8.12	9.19
Improved water sources (% population with access)	80.58	86.71	91.96	95.89
Physicians (per 1,000 people)	1.29	1.43	1.74	2.20
Health expenditure per capita (US$)	463.50	821.14	1,234.27	1,658.48
Prevalence of undernourishment (% population)	16.10	13.70	10.04	6.71
Mortality rate, infant (per 1,000 live births)	57.80	41.40	28.92	23.44
Life expectancy at birth (years)	66.85	69.63	72.24	74.18
Population growth (annual %)	1.43	1.24	1.19	1.29
Internet Users (per 100 people)	1.70	20.00	51.70	92.76

0% 20% 40% 60% 80% 100%

■ 1997   □ 2007   ■ 2017   □ 2027

Figure 3. Where we are losing or there is no progress

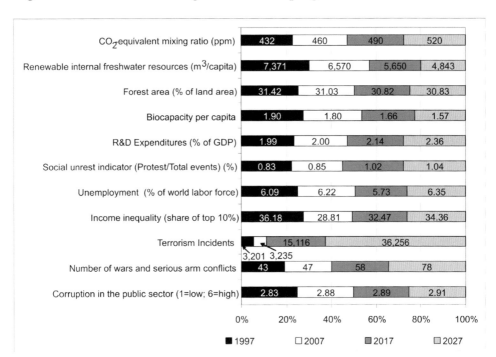

Although we are winning more than losing, where we are losing is very serious. "Business as usual" trend projections for water, food, unemployment, terrorism, organized crime, and pollution could create complex future disasters. Humanity has the means to avoid these disasters and build a great future, but too many of the necessary decisions and cultural changes to improve our prospects are not being made.

Even though the most significant of the world's challenges and solutions are global in nature, global foresight and global-scale decisionmaking systems are rarely used. Global governance systems are not keeping up with growing global interdependence.

However, global decisionmaking may show signs of improvement with the implementation of the Paris Agreement on Climate Change, the UN 2030 Agenda for Sustainable Development, and advances in the International

Organization for Standardization, the World Health Organization, and other international bodies.

"The United Nations Sustainable Development Goals (SDGs) and the Paris Climate Agreement provide the most powerful common agenda the world has ever seen for achieving peace and prosperity on a healthy planet."
                                                    —The UN Global Compact

15 Global Challenges

The 15 Global Challenges provide a framework to assess the global and local prospects for humanity. The Challenges are interdependent: an improvement in one makes it easier to address others; deterioration in one makes it harder to address others. Arguing whether one is more important than another is like arguing that the human nervous system is more important than the respiratory system.

Figure 4. Global Challenges

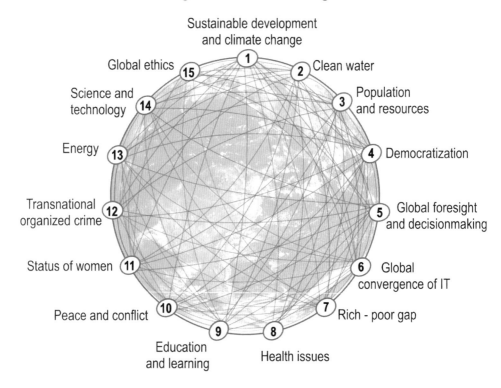

1.

GLOBAL CHALLENGES

Through a series 55 global futures research studies (beginning in 1997) and global scanning systems, The Millennium Project has identified and been updating 15 Global Challenges. These can be used both as a framework to understand global change and as an agenda to improve the future. The online Global Futures Intelligence System has a more complete assessment of the 15 Global Challenges than the very short overviews in this chapter.

These Challenges are transnational in nature and transinstitutional in solution. They cannot be addressed by any government or institution acting alone. They require collaborative action among governments, international organizations, corporations, universities, NGOs, and creative individuals. There is greater consensus about the global situation as expressed in these Challenges and the actions to address them than is evident in the news media.

Although listed in sequence, Challenge 1 on sustainable development and climate change is no more or less important than Challenge 15 on global ethics. The graphs used in this chapter illustrate trends for several variables and developments that assess changes relevant to the Global Challenges presented. They were created using the State of the Future Index methodology.

Each Global Challenge in GFIS has much more information updated in real time in GFIS at https://themp.org, where each Challenge has the following menu:

1. Situation Chart: Current situation, desired situation, and policies to address the gap
2. Report: Short overview (slightly more detailed than presented in this chapter) plus regional considerations, continuously updated, followed by more detailed content, suggested actions, and other relevant information, totaling the equivalent of some 100–300 pages (depending on the Challenge)
3. Digest: Dashboard-like display of latest information related to each Challenge
4. Edits: Latest edits to the reports and situation charts
5. Scanning: Important information with potential impact to the respective Challenge
6. News: Latest news relevant to the Challenge
7. Comments: Invites users to make comments or ask questions
8. Models: Interactive computer models that can show trends of the Challenge
9. Resources: Web resources for further information on the subject of the respective Challenge
10. Books: Books relevant to the subject of the respective Challenge
11. Papers: Papers relevant to the subject of the respective Challenge
12. Questions: A blog-like area where subscribers and reviewers discuss issues they would like to explore
13. Data: Data sets relevant to the respective Challenge

Figure 1.1 shows screenshot of the GFIS Situation Chart for Challenge 3, Population and Resources:

Figure 1.1 Screenshot of the GFIS Challenge 3 Situation Chart

Readers are invited to contribute their insights to improve the overview of these 15 global challenges for future editions. Please email us at <info@millennium-project.org> or subscribe to the Global Futures Intelligence System at www.themp.org to participate in the full system.

GLOBAL CHALLENGE 1: HOW CAN SUSTAINABLE DEVELOPMENT BE ACHIEVED FOR ALL WHILE ADDRESSING GLOBAL CLIMATE CHANGE?

Some 252 million years ago, global warming due to increased atmospheric CO_2 that led to ocean current changes, increases in hydrogen sulfate (H_2S), and ozone depletion killed 97% of life during the Permian extinction. This could happen again unless we learn how to turn around the growing greenhouse gas emissions and reduce the volume already in the atmosphere today.[1] According to NASA, 16 of the 17 warmest years on record occurred since 2001.

The Paris Agreement on Climate Change, with 197 Parties to the Convention, that went into force in November 2016 calls for efforts to cap temperature increases to 1.5°C (2.7°F) above pre-industrial levels. Even though the growth in CO_2 emissions has slowed over the past three years due to efficiencies and a move away from coal by the U.S. and China, the accumulative effect continues warming Earth.[2]

According to NASA the global temperature has already increased by 0.94°C (1.7°F) since 1880 and sea levels have risen 8–9 inches during the same period. If current trends continue, the 2017 US Climate Report projects an increase of 2.8–4.8°C (5–7.5°F) increase by 2100. Sea levels are rising at 3.4 millimeters per year and ocean acidity is projected to increase 100–150% over pre-industrial levels by the end of this century.

Turning around GHG growth will require unprecedented global efforts since today's 7.5 billion world population is expected to grow by another 2 billion by 2050 and the global economy is expected to triple during this same period.

Although the CO_2 equivalent of 450 ppm is the politically acceptable cap, some argue it should be 350 ppm since we already see massive impacts today with 410 ppm, so why would 450 be sustainable? We have to reduce not only

---

[1] Peter Ward, *Under Green Sky*, https://www.amazon.com/Under-Green-Sky-Warming-Extinctions/dp/0061137928.
[2] International Energy Agency, https://www.iea.org/newsroom/news/2017/march/iea-finds-co2-emissions-flat-for-third-straight-year-even-as-global-economy-grew.html.

GHG emissions but also the volume of GHGs already in the atmosphere today. The Paris Convention on Climate Change and country pledges should be enforceable through boycotts, sanctions, and other means. Global citizens should understand that Earth does not possess infinite resources; that the Earth is a Closed-Loop System that should be applied to various economic, political, and environmental management systems; that consumption and waste management will have to change; and that environmental sustainability is a top economic, social value, and political priority.

World leaders have agreed to achieve 17 UN Sustainable Development Goals with 169 sub-goals by 2030.[3]

Actions to Address Global Challenge 1:
- U.S.-China Apollo-Like Goal, with a NASA-Like R&D program to achieve it, that others can join; if U.S. falters, then an EU-China Goal should be pursued.
- Produce meat, milk, leather, and other animal products directly from genetic materials without growing animals: Saves energy, land, water, health costs, and greenhouse gases.
- Seawater/saltwater agriculture.
- Increase vegetarian diets.
- Retrofit older cities to Eco-smart Cities and build new additions as Eco-smart Cities.
- Continue policies that reduce fertility rates in high population growth areas.
- Reduce energy per unit of GDP.
- Increase forest coverage.
- Transition from fossil to renewable energy sources (see Global Challenge 13 for more detail and http://www.go100re.net/map for current global status).
- Introduce cap-and-trade systems.

---

[3] See http://www.un.org/sustainabledevelopment/ and progress, https://unstats.un.org/sdgs/files/report/2017/TheSustainableDevelopmentGoalsReport2017.pdf.

- Establish carbon taxes.
- Engage arts/media/entertainment to foster work/lifestyle changes.
- Train community resilience teams.
- Make long-range coastal evacuation and migration plans.
- Evaluate geo-engineering options.

For more information, including regional considerations in Africa, Asia, Europe, Latin America, and North America, click on Short Overview at: https://themp.org, Challenge 1, "Report" section.

Figure 1.2 GHG emissions, CO2-equivalent mixing ratio (ppm)

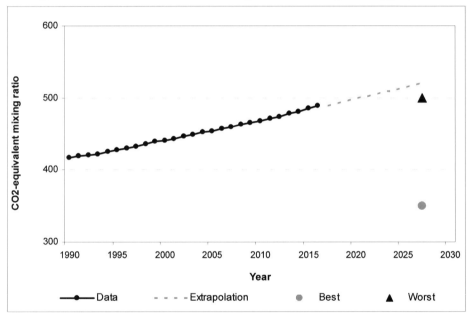

Source: NOAA Earth System Research Laboratory, with Millennium Project compilation and forecast

GLOBAL CHALLENGE 2: HOW CAN EVERYONE HAVE SUFFICIENT CLEAN WATER WITHOUT CONFLICT?

Over 90% of the world now has access to improved drinking water, up from 76% in 1990. That is an improvement for 2.3 billion people in less than 20 years. However, that still leaves 884 million people without access, an increase from 663 million in 2015. Water consumption for about 500 million people is twice what can be renewed by nature, water tables are falling on all continents, the volume of untreated wastewater increases every year, and about 80% of all wastewater is discharged without treatment.[4] Nearly half of humanity gets its water from sources controlled by two or more countries. In drier regions, global warming will increase droughts; in more humid regions, global warming will increase flooding. A third of humanity does not have access to a proper toilet or latrine, and 892 million people still defecate in the open.

Humanity uses 70% of its water supply for agriculture, 20% for industry, and 10% for domestic uses; however, the more developed nations use 50-80% of their water supply for industry. As the developing world expands its industries, agriculture, and population growth, and as GDP per capita income rises, water consumption per capita will increase, making it impossible to avoid serious water crises and migrations unless major changes occur.

World leaders have agreed to create universal access to safe water and sanitation and other related UN Sustainable Development Goals by 2030.[5]

Actions to Address Global Challenge 2:
- Increase R&D for lower cost of desalination.
- Invest in the development of wastewater products such as fertilizer, algae (for biofuel and feeding shrimp), and recovering nitrogen and phosphorus.
- Implement WHO and UNESCO plans for universal water and sanitation access.

---

[4] UN, *World Water Development Report 2017*,
http://unesdoc.unesco.org/images/0024/002475/247552e.pdf.
[5] See http://www.un.org/sustainabledevelopment/water-and-sanitation/.

- Manage all aspects of water resources to promote efficiency, equity, and sustainable development (integrated water management).
- Create and promote smart phone apps to show water used to make products.
- Produce animal products from genetic materials without growing animals.
- Invest in seawater/saltwater agricultural development.
- Promote Increased vegetarian diets.
- Mass-produce electrochemical wastewater treatment solar power toilets.
- Develop point-of-use water-purification technology.

For more information, including regional considerations, see the Short Overview at: https://themp.org, Challenge 2, "Report" section.

Figure 1.3 Renewable internal freshwater resources per capita (cubic meters)

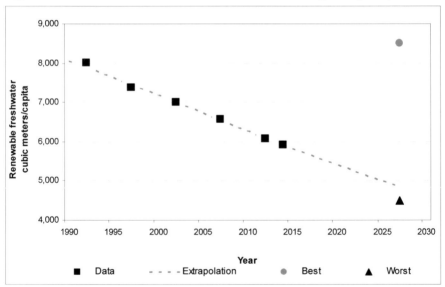

Source: World Bank indicators, with Millennium Project compilation and forecast

GLOBAL CHALLENGE 3: HOW CAN POPULATION GROWTH AND RESOURCES BE BROUGHT INTO BALANCE?

The current world population of 7.6 billion is expected to grow by another 2.2 billion in just 33 years (by 2050).[6] If all are to be fed, then food production will have to increase 50%[7] over production in 2012, while urban areas are expected to triple in size by 2030, resulting in a loss of peri-urban farmlands. With improvements in child survival, and its synergy with enhanced family planning improvements, this population growth could be lower.[8] Life expectancy at birth increased from 46 years in 1950 to 67 years in 2010 and 71.5 years in 2015. In 2017 there were 962 million people aged 60 or older; the UN projects this to grow to 2.2 billion by 2050.[9]

This aging effect is one aspect of highly varied population age structures across countries stemming from their widely differing historical population growth, now moving to the future.[10] (The continuing and future strain (and potential gain) of internal/urbanization and international migration is another development, driven in part by economic, political. and religious effects of high population growth, age structure, and available resources.)[11] The uneven advances and implementation of health care, the variations in family planning and changing reproductive behavior, and the devastations of war, disease, and famine have left some countries with disproportionately aging populations and others with an overabundance of children and young people compared with workers and retirees. While this has been ongoing, the impacts and capacity to reshape economies and societies will become

---

[6] United Nations, *World Population Prospects: The 2017 Revision*, http://www.un.org/en/development/desa/population/events/pdf/other/21/21June_FINAL%20PRESS%20RELEASE_WPP17.pdf.
[7] FAO, *Future of Food and Agriculture: Trends and Challenges*, http://www.fao.org/3/a-i6583e.pdf page 46; however, this does not calculate full balanced nutrition.
[8] https://www.ted.com/talks/hans_rosling_on_global_population_growth#t-523265.
[9] https://www.un.org/development/desa/publications/world-population-prospects-the-2017-revision.html.
[10] John May, *World Population Policies: Their Origin, Evolution, and Impact*, Springer.
[11] *Why Population Matters to Migration AND Urbanization*, https://pai.org/wp-content/uploads/2012/.../PAI-1293-MIGRATION.

increasingly visible—for some, strains on labor and productivity to support the growing proportion of elderly (for instance, in most of Europe and countries of the previous Soviet Union); for others, challenges in the means to educate young people while addressing their frustration, anger, and unrest if expectations for employment and better life are not met (for instance, most of Africa and much of Latin America). The China that for 50 years harvested development from its large and growing youthful low-wage population now faces a future of lower population growth where those same workers are retired, straining the proportionately fewer workers that follow them and putting pressure on continued high rates of technological change to sustain progress.[12]

Advances in longevity R&D are likely to help many more people live much longer and healthier lives than current trends. This includes regenerative medicine, DNA repair, and other longevity research. For example, scanning ultrasound removes amyloid-β and restores memory in 75% of Alzheimer's diseased rats. If this and other related research can work on humans, then older people could be an economic asset rather than a liability. Such advances will be needed; otherwise the long-term future health costs of an aging society cannot be met. Human brain projects, artificial intelligence, and other advances are likely to eventually prevent mental deterioration in old age and even increase intelligence. People will work past current retirement age and create many forms of work. This will reduce the economic burden on younger generations and provide a more interesting life for the elderly.

However, the world is not creating Eco-smart Cities and retrofitting older cities fast enough to prevent future large-scale complex disasters from decaying infrastructures for water, energy, waste, transportation, housing, food, and security. Urban populations will nearly double by 2050, increasing the pressure on these systems especially in developing-country cities, where nearly all of the population growth will occur. AI connected to IoT and sensor networks will be needed to provide real-time information for

---

[12] http://www.economist.com/node/21555533.

continual urban repair, improvement, and public participation. Early examples are Songdo in South Korea and Masdar City in Abu Dhabi. India plans to build 100 smart cities by 2022. China has launched nearly 200 smart city pilot projects. People are moving around the planet more than ever; 244 million people moved from one country to another during 2015.[13] Future migrations from low-income, high-youth-employment regions to high-income aging societies seem inevitable.

Unless agriculture and food production change, the environmental impacts of feeding another 2.2 billion people by 2050 plus improved nutrition for a billion undernourished today will be devastating. Agricultural runoffs are already polluting rivers and creating dead zones around the world. Factory farming is increasing food-borne diseases. Malnourishment is falling, but slowly from 19% some 25 years ago to about 11% today, although infant mortality for children under five has been cut in half over the same time period. About 800 million are still hungry.[14] Meanwhile, at least 41 million children under five, including 10 million in Africa, are overweight or obese. See Challenge 2 for implications for water resources and Challenge 13 for energy resources.

Actions to Address Global Challenge 3:
- Support policies to improve child survival, family planning, and girls' education.
- Improve methods that strengthen age differential intergenerational transfers to secure skills and employment for youth and care and services for the elderly.
- Implement the UN Urban Agenda.[15]

---

[13] http://www.un.org/en/development/desa/population/migration/publications/wallchart/docs/MigrationWallChart2015.pdf.

[14] *UN Sustainable Development Goals Report 2016,* https://unstats.un.org/sdgs/report/2016/The%20Sustainable%20Development%20Goals%20Report%202016.pdf.

[15] http://habitat3.org/wp-content/uploads/N1639668-English.pdf.

- Integrate urban sensors, mesh networks, and intelligent software to create smarter cities that let citizens help in urban improvements.
- Increase training in resilience, disaster forecasting, and management.
- Teach urban systems ecology.
- Increase R&D in saltwater agriculture (halophytes) on coastlines to produce food for humans and animals, biofuels, and pulp for the paper industry as well as to absorb CO_2, which also reduces the drain on freshwater agriculture and increases employment.
- Improve rain-fed agriculture and irrigation management.
- Invest in precision agriculture and aquaculture.
- Produce pure meat without growing animals (demonstrated in 2013).
- Genetic engineering for higher-yielding and drought-tolerant crops.
- Reduce food losses from farm to mouth (one-third or 1.3 billion tons of agricultural production is wasted each year).[16]
- Plant sea grass to bring back wild fish populations along the coastlines.
- Expand insect production for animal feed and human diets (insects have low environmental impact per nutrition, and 2 billion people already supplement their diet with insects today).
- Encourage vegetarianism.
- Build floating cities for ocean wind & solar energy, agriculture, and fish farms.
- Accelerate R&D for safe nanotechnology to help reduce material use per unit of output while increasing quality.

For more information, including regional considerations in Africa, Asia, Europe, Latin America, and North America, see the Short Overview at: https://themp.org, Challenge 3, "Report" section.

---

[16] http://www.fao.org/save-food/resources/keyfindings/en/.

Figure1.4 Prevalence of undernourishment (% of population)

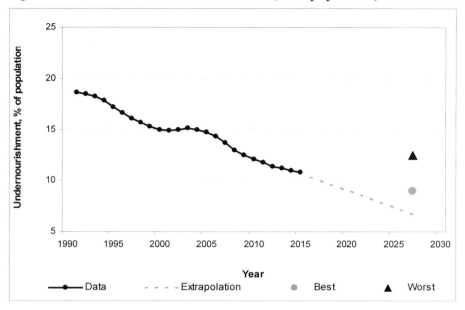

Source: World Bank indicators, with Millennium Project compilation and forecast

GLOBAL CHALLENGE 4: HOW CAN GENUINE DEMOCRACY EMERGE FROM AUTHORITARIAN REGIMES?

New Internet capabilities provide more access for greater participation in governance and are increasingly exposing corruption. Synergistically self-organized human rights movements for sustainable global democratic systems are taking place all over the world. At the same time, anti-democratic forces are increasingly using new cyber tools to manipulate democratic processes. The long-term growth of democratization has stalled over the past decade. Freedom House[17] reported that 105 countries are experiencing a net decline in freedom while 61 are improving in net freedom and that 67 countries declined in political rights and civil liberties while 36 registered gains. Of the 195 countries assessed, 87 were rated free, 59 partly free, and 49 (36% of the world's population) not free.

Although the perceptions and implementations of democracy differ globally, it is generally accepted that democracy is a relationship between a responsible citizenry and a responsive government that encourages participation in the political process and guarantees basic rights. Reinforcing this globally are NGOs like Transparency International and the intergovernmental organizations like the Open Government Partnership created in 2011. OGP has grown to 75 national and 15 subnational governments that have agreed to 2,500 commitments to promote transparency, empower citizens, fight corruption, and harness new technologies to strengthen governance. Global trends are also reinforcing this, such as the increasing interdependencies, changing nature of power, increasingly educated publics, growing mobility and solidarity of people worldwide, and the need to collectively address major planetary existential challenges. However, democratization is threatened by increasingly sophisticated organized crime, terrorism, corruption, fake news, and other cyber manipulation of elections and the electorate.

---

[17] Freedom House, *Freedom in the World 2017*, https://freedomhouse.org/report/freedom-world/freedom-world-2017.

Actions to Address Global Challenge 4:

- Secure tamper-proof electoral systems.
- Invest in R&D that could counter fake news.
- Establish international standards and agreements for the digital world.
- Implement global strategies to counter organized crime.
- Establish and enforce measures to reduce corruption.
- Promote transparency, participation, inclusion, and accountability in decisionmaking.
- Support research to get unfair influence of large sums of money out of politics.
- Promote new forms of e-governance.
- Require civics in all forms of education.
- Explore new forms like Liquid Democracy[18] and Democracy 4.0.
- Develop standards that support democratic values.
- Produce cash flow projections for guaranteed basic income.
- Implement UN treaties on minorities, migrants, and refugees.
- Include 10 lessons from Devex research: move forward incrementally when beginning a democratic transition; retain a positive and inclusive vision at all times; build coalitions; create and protect spaces for dialogue; focus on constitution building; manage eventual tensions; understand the importance of political parties; deal carefully with military, security, and intelligence services; recognize the need for real reconciliation and transitional justice; and bring the gender lens to democratic transitions.

For more information, including regional considerations in Africa, Asia, Europe, Latin America, and North America, see the Short Overview at: https://themp.org, Challenge 4, "Report" section.

---

[18] https://medium.com/organizer-sandbox/liquid-democracy-true-democracy-for-the-21st-century-7c66f5e53b6f.

Figure 1.5 Freedom rights (number of countries rated "free")

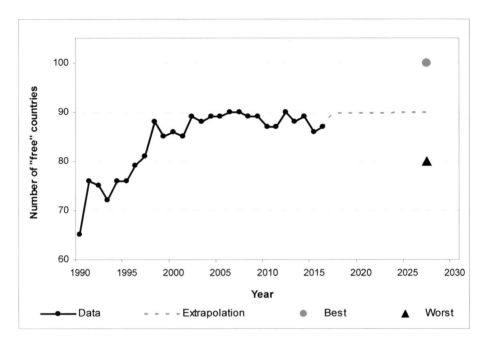

Source: Freedom House, with Millennium Project compilation and forecast

GLOBAL CHALLENGE 5: HOW CAN DECISIONMAKING BE ENHANCED BY INTEGRATING IMPROVED GLOBAL FORESIGHT DURING UNPRECEDENTED ACCELERATING CHANGE?

Although the most significant of the world's challenges and solutions are global in nature, global foresight and global-scale decisionmaking systems are rarely employed. Global governance systems are not keeping up with growing global interdependence. Since governments and large corporations have to make decisions taking into account global changes that are beyond their control, many are creating future strategy or foresight units[19] to contribute to their strategic planning. Finland created a permanent Parliamentary Committee on the Future in 1993 to support government foresight and decisionmaking.

Decisionmakers are rarely trained in foresight and decisionmaking, even though decision support and foresight systems are constantly being improved with artificial intelligence, big data analytics, simulations, collective intelligence systems, e-governance participatory systems, and a deeper understanding of psychological factors that impinge on decisionmaking and its outcomes[20] and as mobile apps proliferate.

Futures research is the systematic exploration of assumptions about future possibilities; unfortunately, its work has not been systematically evaluated and applied to improve its quality and to demonstrate its effect on decisionmaking. Instead, the tyranny of the moment tends to overrule long-term global perspectives. Short-term, selfish, economic decisionmaking can be blamed for the 2008 global financial crisis, continued environmental degradation, and widening income disparities. The long-term goal to land on the moon accelerated technological innovations and economic growth and lifted the human spirit. The long-term goal to eradicate smallpox inspired many people to cooperate across cultural and political divides. A U.S.-China long-term goal on climate change could inspire even greater international collaborations.

---

[19] See Review of 28 Government Future Strategy Units (see Governance and Future in the Research section of Governance and Futures); Intro to that study: https://themp.org/#group_id=522529690d6eaeb742001664&section=report.
[20] See Daniel Kahneman, *Thinking, Fast and Slow*, Farrar, Straus and Giroux.

Humanity needs a global, multifaceted, general long-term view of the future with long-range goals to facilitate contemporary decisions that lead to a brighter future, and this requires a means for linking research agendas and R&D to those goals. The UN Sustainable Development Goals for 2030 provide much of that framework, but we still need to understand the potential consequences and opportunities afforded by accelerating future technological innovations. In the meantime, national foresight and decisionmaking can be improved.

Actions to Address Global Challenge 5:

- Establish a permanent parliamentary "Committee for the Future," as Finland has done, to provide foresight for government and other parliamentary committees.
- Establish or improve future strategy units for heads of state and government.[21]
- Link these government units with corporate, UN, and academic future strategy units to improve international strategic coherence and coordination.
- Create a network of government and nongovernmental futurists on call for quick futures assessments (Real-Time Delphi software could support this).
- Compute and publish annual national and global State of the Future Indexes.
- Develop national online collective intelligence systems on the future of the nation, with public access.
- Create a classified collective intelligence system for the heads of government connected to related units in government to offer the opportunity of some continuity in national long-term strategy from one administration to the next.

---

[21] Some of these suggestions were drawn from *Anticipatory Governance*, a detailed report on analysis and recommendations prepared for the U.S. White House, available at https://dl.dropboxusercontent.com/u/44303479/Anticipatory_Governance_Practical_Upgrades.pdf.

- Synthesize relevant futures research for an annual State of the Future report for nations, issues, sectors, and/or organizations.
- Include 5–10 year allocations in government budgets based on rolling 5–10 year SOFIs, scenarios, and strategies.
- Advisors to decisionmakers should participate in the informal long-term strategy networks to share and learn best practices.
- Require a "future considerations" section in policy reporting requirements.
- Create institutions that teach decision-making; the curriculum could include foresight, risk, uncertainty, psychology, game theory, successful historical decision situations, and potential future crises.
- Add foresight as a performance evaluation criteria for senior government officials.
- Include how to connect foresight to decisionmaking in government training programs.[22]
- Test proposed policies before implementation by postulating random future events of all sorts and evaluating how these might affect the policies.[23]
- Teach decisionmaking, foresight, futures research, and synthesis as well as analysis throughout educational systems.
- Fund convergence among disciplines to address global challenges.
- Create stronger links between R&D budgets and priority of problems that need solving.

For more information, including regional considerations in Africa, Asia, Europe, Latin America, and North America, see the Short Overview at: https://themp.org, Challenge 5, "Report" section.

---

[22] Factors Required for Successful Implementation of Futures Research in Decisionmaking, which includes a 26-item checklist in Research Section of GFIS in Governance and Futures, at https://themp.org/#group_id=522529690d6eaeb742001664&section=report.
[23] See prototype at http://www.changesignals.com (code: whatif)).

GLOBAL CHALLENGE 6: HOW CAN GLOBAL INFORMATION & COMMUNICATIONS TECHNOLOGIES ALONG WITH MACHINE INTELLIGENCE, BIG DATA, AND CLOUD COMPUTING WORK FOR EVERYONE?

Some 51% of the world—over 3.8 billion people—are now connected to the Internet. About two-thirds of the people in the world have a mobile phone; over half have smart phones. The continued development and proliferation of smart phone apps are putting state-of-the-art AI systems in the palm of many hands around the world. The race is on to complete the global nervous system of civilization and make supercomputing power and artificial intelligence available to everyone. The human brain projects of U.S., EU, China, and other countries, plus corporate AI research, should lead to augmented individual human and collective intelligence. Some $15 billion was invested in 2,250 AI business deals between 2012 and 2016, while robotics got $3 billion invested in 488 deals.[24] China has declared its goal of being the world's AI leader by 2030.[25]

How well governments develop and coordinate Internet security technology and regulations may determine the future quality of cyberspace. Malware attacks are increasing. As of 2017, more advertising money is spent on Internet than on television, and half of all Internet traffic is via mobile phones. Rapidly increasing video, AR/VR, and IoT use raises concerns about anticipating and meeting future bandwidth demands for an Internet infrastructure not designed for these applications but whose reliability has become strategically vital for much of civilization. Over a billion hours are viewed each day on YouTube. With the evolution of the Internet of Things, wearable computers, autonomous vehicles, and brain-computer interfaces, cyber security will become increasingly important. Data need to be encrypted at all levels. Low-cost computers are replacing high-cost weapons as an instrument of power in asymmetrical cyber and information warfare. Information security has to address a wide and diverse range of "enemies"—

---

[24] https://www.cbinsights.com/reports/CB-Insights_State-of-AI-Report.pdf.
[25] State Council of China's three-step blueprint to be AI leader by 2030, http://tech.qq.com/a/20170720/045464.htm.

from the "geek in the back room" to criminal organizations and governments.

Blockchain is being explored as a new approach to IoT security, as is quantum entanglement. Quantum cryptography is an emerging security technology in which two parties can generate shared, secret cryptographic material between ground stations or between Earth and satellite (as demonstrated in June 2017 by China). All this is leading one day to a global-scale quantum Internet.[26]

As the Fourth Industrial Revolution evolves, all elements of a business will become connected with artificial intelligence; companies will increasingly become collective intelligence systems. Financial services and other kinds of businesses could just become software. The three kinds of artificial intelligence are artificial narrow, single-purpose intelligence (what we have today); artificial general intelligence, adaptable to multiple purposes re-writing its own code (which might not be possible, but some expect it by 2030); and artificial super intelligence, general intelligence that sets its own goals independent of humans (what science fiction warns about). Some unemployment impacts of narrow AI are being seen today, but if artificial general intelligence can be created, then the big impacts on unemployment, economics, and culture will much greater. Facebook closed down AI bots that created their own language that humans could not understand, and Google's AutoML can create new AI better and faster than humans, using layers of neural networks.[27]

Who owns the intellectual property of AI produced by AI with participation of many inputs from humans and sensors around the world? How can standards, certification, and testing keep up with AI when humans will no longer know completely how it works? Meanwhile, tele-everything continues to grow. Over 700 universities offered 6,850 tele-education MOOCs to 58 million students during 2016. Global telemedicine was valued

[26] https://www.nature.com/articles/ncomms15971.
[27] Google I/O Keynote by Sundar Pichai, CEO Google
https://www.youtube.com/watch?v=Y2VF8tmLFHw.

at approximately $18.20 billion in 2016 and is expected to reach approximately $38 billion by 2022.

Actions to Address Global Challenge 6:

- Make Internet access a right of citizenship, as Finland did in 2010.
- Support Google's and Facebook's efforts to give universal Internet access to the world, regardless of location.
- Establish international agreements on IoT security standards and patchability.
- Explore elements for a global agreement on use and future development of machine learning and use of artificial intelligence.
- Create public global collective intelligence systems for water, energy, food, S&T, etc. and connect them in a global system (www.themp.org is an early example).
- Create low-cost hand-held computers with direct satellite access for low-income regions to access educational software and telephony, with elementary literacy as a first priority.
- Train everyone in their roles in cyber security and stewardship.
- Invent synergies between government cyber security personnel and independent hackers for a safer Internet.
- Promote tele-nations and tele-citizens: people from poorer nations who live and work in richer nations who help develop their original countries via volunteer telecommuting.

For more information, including regional considerations in Africa, Asia, Europe, Latin America, and North America, see the Short Overview at: https://themp.org, Challenge 6, "Report" section.

Figure 1.6 Internet users (per 100 people)

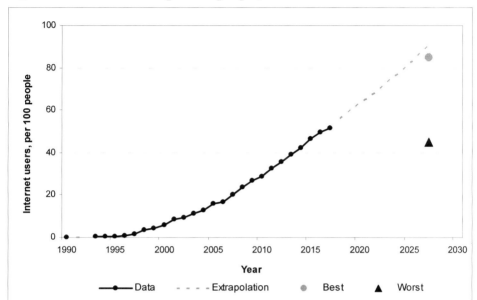

Source: World Bank indicators and Internetworldstats, with Millennium
Project compilation and forecast

GLOBAL CHALLENGE 7: HOW CAN ETHICAL MARKET ECONOMIES BE ENCOURAGED TO HELP REDUCE THE GAP BETWEEN RICH AND POOR?

Extreme poverty fell from 51% in 1981 to 13% in 2012 and less than 10% today,[28] mostly due to income growth in China and India.[29] However, inequality in Africa remains a serious threat to future stability, with four of the five most unequal countries in the world found there.[30] UNDP's Multidimensional Poverty Index applied to 102 developing countries found about 1.5 million people living in multidimensional poverty.[31] World leaders have agreed to achieve the UN Sustainable Development Goal of eliminating extreme poverty by 2030.

Meanwhile, the concentration of wealth is increasing (the wealth of just 8 billionaires equals that of 3.6 billion people, the poorer half of humanity), income gaps are widening, employment-less economic growth continues, return on investment in capital and technology is usually better than on labor, and future technologies can replace much of human labor; hence, long-term structural unemployment seems inevitable unless new approaches to economics and the nature of work are created (See Chapter 4 on *Future Work/Tech 2050 Global Scenarios and Strategies*). Historically, inequality has been addressed through such mechanisms as war, revolution, debt relief, legal system reforms, tax adjustments, and land redistribution.

Since artificial intelligence will reproduce and learn faster than humans, its universal proliferation seems inevitable. Algorithms are already out-performing humans in driving cars, face recognition, complex games, and even some forms of medical diagnosis. AI and other next technologies should lower costs of education, transportation, and medical care and should provide new tax income from taxing robots and other next technologies,

---

[28] UN Sustainable Development Goals Report 2016, https://unstats.un.org/sdgs/report/2016/The%20Sustainable%20Development%20Goals%20Report%202016.pdf.
[29] The World Bank now defines extreme poverty as those living under $1.90/day and moderate poverty as those living between $3.10/day and $1.90/day.
[30] World Bank, GINI Dataset, http://www.worldbank.org/en/research/brief/all-the-ginis.
[31] UNDP, *Multidimensional Poverty Index*, http://hdr.undp.org/en/content/multidimensional-poverty-index-mpi.

making universal basic income financially sustainable possibly by 2030 (see scenarios in Chapter 4). Finland, Canada, and others are conducting pilot UBI experiments.

Although income gaps between rich and poor individuals are widening, the gap between nations is expected to narrow. Emerging market and developing economies are growing around 4–5% annually, while more advanced countries are growing closer to 2%. IMF expects growth of the world economy to increase from 3.1% percent in 2016 to 3.5% in 2017 and 3.6% in 2018.[32] Given population growth at 1.11%, global income per capita is growing 2.39% annually.

Actions to Address Global Challenge 7:

- Poorer regions should be assisted in investing more in developing finished products for export and extending local value chains instead of relying on commodities and "leapfrogging" to more advanced technology.
- Raise minimum wages and address executive wages.
- Consider seriously new progressively equalizing instruments, e.g. wealth tax and revising inheritance laws.
- Counter entrenched privilege.
- Promote Decentralized Autonomous Organizations[33] for an unlimited number of peer-to-peer ad hoc "workers."
- Explore guaranteed income programs, as next technologies may lead to long-term structural unemployment, and create cash flow projections to explore financial sustainability of universal basic income.
- Tax next technologies for new income to social support systems and create tax systems that ensure big business and wealthy individuals pay their fair share.

---

[32] GDP may be a more useful measure for industrial economies than information economies. For example, the millions of people searching billions of computer pages totaling more than a trillion searches per year are not counted in GDP.
[33] https://en.wikipedia.org/wiki/Decentralized_autonomous_organization.

- Invest in Kickstarter-like crowd sourcing to reduce the concentration of wealth.
- Explore alternative transaction systems like blockchain and cryptocurrencies (over 850 cryptocurrencies with $145 trillion (not billion) market capitalization).[34]
- Explore global workforce sourcing solutions that overcome immigration and migration barriers to allow qualified workers to move where they can meet the vacant skilled labor requirements.
- Expand micro-credit and small business credit systems and business training.
- Conduct training programs on how to use mobile phone Internet access to find and develop markets worldwide instead of looking for non-existent local jobs.
- Establish community centers for access and training for self-employed to use advanced technology like 3D printing, AI/robotics, and AI apps.
- The capital requirements for start-ups are increasingly low—consider YouTube, Facebook, Uber, etc.
- Increase emphasis on science, technology, engineering, and mathematics education and lifelong learning and retraining.
- Create mechanisms to help people invest in automations that replace their job; e.g., truck drivers manage and invest into ownership of driverless trucks.
- Create personal AI/Avatars to support self-employment.
- Give greater attention to the frontiers for work related to the forthcoming biological revolution, which may be as large as or larger than the industrial or information revolutions.
- Establish Labor/Business/Government Next Technologies databases.

---

[34] https://coinmarketcap.com/currencies/.

For more information, including regional considerations in Africa, Asia, Europe, Latin America, and North America, see the Short Overview at: https://themp.org, Challenge 7, "Report" section.

Figure 1.7 Economic income inequality (Income share held by highest 10%)

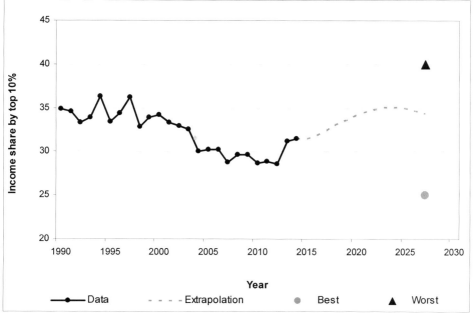

Source: World Bank indicators, with Millennium Project compilation and forecast

GLOBAL CHALLENGE 8: HOW CAN THE THREAT OF NEW AND REEMERGING DISEASES AND IMMUNE MICROORGANISMS BE REDUCED?

The health of humanity continues to improve; life expectancy at birth increased globally from 46 years in 1950 to 67 years in 2010 and 71.5 years in 2015. Total mortality from infectious disease fell from 25% in 1998 to 15.9% in 2015[35]. Children are receiving the highest level of routine immunization coverage in history.[36] Indigenous measles and rubella have been eliminated from the Americas, and maternal and neonatal tetanus have been eliminated in Southeast Asia. Malaria cases decreased by 41% from 2000 to 2015. As the world ages, chronic diseases are increasing (i.e., deaths due to stroke, heart disease, and cancers). However, WHO verified more than 1,100 epidemic events over the past five years, and antimicrobial resistance, malnutrition, and obesity are increasing. TB is the leading infection cause of death globally, with increasing drug resistance. Zika in the Americas and cholera in Yemen (half a million) and Haiti (1 million) continue to spread, while urban yellow fever in Angola and the Democratic Republic of Congo prompted the largest emergency vaccination campaign ever undertaken in Africa—30 million people were successfully vaccinated. WHO is monitoring avian influenza in nearly 50 countries and continues to warn that the world is not prepared for a major epidemic.

The most advanced vaccine for malaria will be tested in 2018 in Ghana, Kenya, and Malawi, while human trials for an HIV vaccine are in progress. HIV/AIDS continues to decrease: about 1.8 million people were infected with HIV in 2016[37], down from 5.4 million in 1999; 1 million died of HIV-related illness in 2016, down from 2 million in 2010; and 19.5 million people with HIV (53%) were on treatment, up from 17.1 million in 2015.

Embryo gene editing has begun and could eventually eliminate inherited disease tendencies, including infectious diseases; however, such editing for human enhancement is quite controversial, and a U.S. National Academy of

---

[35] http://www.who.int/healthinfo/global_burden_disease/estimates/en/index1.html
[36] http://www.who.int/publications/10-year-review/vaccines/en/index2.html.
[37] http://www.unaids.org/en/resources/fact-sheet

Sciences panel has recommended against such research at this time. Regenerative medicine holds the potential to create living, functional cells and tissues extending life, and DNA repair and other longevity research continue.

But investment and development of new antibiotics have not kept pace with current and potential antibiotic resistance around the world. No new classes of antibiotics have come on the market for more than 25 years. A superbug (with mcr-1 gene) resistant to antibiotics now exists on several continents. Making antibiotics much stronger is being explored to prevent drug residence by reducing the time needed to be cured. A universal vaccine to bring up the immune system could become an alternative to slow the process of making new vaccines for new versions of diseases. Genomic vaccines[38] are being tested to inject DNA or RNA into cells to produce a desired protein to help train the immune system to eliminate a selected pathogen. But how should we prioritize funds for infectious diseases? Should it be number of currently infected people or economic impact vs. potential for spread of infection vs. mortality rates? As the aging populations of richer countries are expected to exhaust medical budgets, will China, India, and other growing economies pick up to burden?

Meanwhile, global health research investment has been stagnant or falling since 2009, excluding the billions in emergency funding set aside during the Ebola outbreak. The new U.S. administration proposes to cut funding for global heath by 24% along with local cuts in both NIH and CDC. From 2000 to 2009, global health spending grew an average of 11.4% annually, but it fell to 1.8% annually from 2010 to 2016.[39]

Actions to Address Global Challenge 8:
- Implement WHO Global Vaccine Action Plan.[40]
- Increase support to anticipate and counter drug resistance.

---

[38] https://www.scientificamerican.com/article/genomic-vaccines/.
[39] http://www.healthdata.org/sites/default/files/files/policy_report/FGH/2017/IHME_FGH2016_Technical-Report.pdf.
[40] http://www.who.int/immunization/global_vaccine_action_plan/GVAP_doc_2011_2020/en/.

- Improve global plans and resiliency training to address future major epidemics.
- Create and implement strategies to counter the barriers to developing new classes of antibiotics and bringing them to market.
- Complete mortality records worldwide to improve data base for research; only half of all deaths have recorded causes.
- Increase global health funding to its previous annual increase of about 10%.
- Focus on early detection, accurate reporting, prompt isolation, and transparent information and communications infrastructure.
- Increase tele-medicine and AI diagnostics as the shortage of health workers continues to worsen in poorer regions of the world.
- Increase investment in clean drinking water, sanitation, and hand washing.
- Optimize the use of current health technologies (drugs, devices, biological products, medical and surgical procedures, support systems, and organizational systems) with corporate/NGO partnering for holistic approaches to health care.
- Encourage telemedicine, including online self-diagnosis and AI, expert software.
- Climate change and other global environmental changes are resulting in changes in the magnitude and pattern of risks, underlining the need for increased investment in monitoring and surveillance

For more information, including regional considerations in Africa, Asia, Europe, Latin America, and North America, see the Short Overview at: https://themp.org, Challenge 8, "Report" section.

Figure 1.8 Health expenditure per capita (current $)

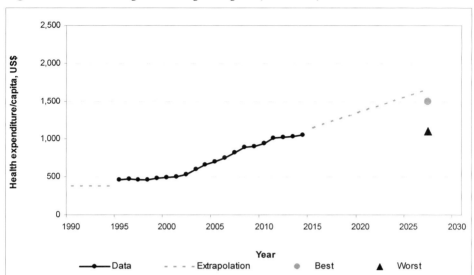

Source: World Bank indicators, with Millennium Project compilation and forecast

GLOBAL CHALLENGE 9. HOW CAN EDUCATION AND LEARNING MAKE HUMANITY MORE INTELLIGENT, KNOWLEDGEABLE, AND WISE ENOUGH TO ADDRESS ITS GLOBAL CHALLENGES?

Artificial Intelligence is being developed to figure out the best ways for you to learn and what you should, need, and/or want to learn. Just as glasses augment our eyes to see better, we will augment our brains to become augmented geniuses; NeuraLink is hiring now to create that, and several companies are testing smart contact lenses and augmented-reality glasses to connect to the IoT. This should speed learning, reduce miscommunications, and make education far more interesting. Much of the world's knowledge is available—either directly or through intermediaries—to the majority of humanity today via many forms of online education. Google and Wikipedia are helping to make the phrase "I don't know" obsolete, and free online self-paced courses proliferate on everything from synthetic biology to elementary arithmetic. Teams led by Facebook and Google are competing to get everyone on the planet connected to the Internet. The price of laptops and smart phones continues to fall, and IoT with data analytics gives real-time precision intelligence. However, successfully applying all these resources to develop wisdom, rather than information pollution, is a huge challenge.

Cognitive/neuroscience and related research has shown that brain performance can be improved by responding to feedback, providing consistency of love and social-emotional support within a diversity of environments, nutrition, reasoning exercises, the belief it is possible (placebo effect), personal contact with intelligent people or via VR simulations, responsible use of software systems and gaming, neuro-pharmacology (enhanced brain chemistry), and memes on classroom walls and elsewhere (e.g., intelligence is sexy). Sufficient sleep, and low-stress, stimulating environments, with certain music, colors, and fragrances, improves concentration and performance. Longer-term future approaches to improving brain performance include reverse engineering the brain such as national brain projects in the U.S., EU, China, and others; applied epigenetics and genetic engineering; and microbes via synthetic biology to eat the plaque on neurons of the elderly.

Meanwhile, innovations are occurring inside and outside of classrooms across the world. Finland plans to use an interdisciplinary approach to teach events and phenomena instead of subjects. China plans to make 3D printers available in its 400,000 elementary schools in two years.[41] South Korea uses telepresence robots with remote native speakers to teach English. Dubai uses 3D glass, holograms, and VR for immersive learning. As neuroscience and psychology improve, their research results can inform teaching strategies.[42] Curriculum design can take into account that students remember most clearly items taught first and last; give frequent, formative (ungraded/low stakes) assessments; allow student opportunities for meta-cognitive reflection on learning/performance; teach students to self-test when studying (simply re-reading notes hurts student long-term learning); emphasize the importance of sleep in learning/memory consolidation; make sure students understand their ability to improve their own brains (neuroplasticity and placebo effect); give students opportunities for choice in learning (enhances engagement/intrinsic motivation); make sure students and teachers understand the effects of stress, fear, and fatigue on higher-order reasoning and memory; allow opportunities to transfer learning through visual/performing arts; help students understand the role of brain anatomy in learning; use immersive virtual and augmented reality devices; and allow frequent opportunities to play.

Because technological capacities available to the individual will be far more powerful than in the past, increased attention has to be given to ethics, values, citizen responsibilities, and noble behavior. And because humanity is becoming far more connected and globalized, special attention should be given to world and macro history, while learning one's own culture and civilization.

---

[41] https://3dprint.com/56699/china-3d-printers-schools/.
[42] Distilled from Glenn Whitman and Ian Kelleher, *Neuroteach: Brain Science and the Future of Education.*

Actions to Address Global Challenge 9:

- Make increasing individual and collective intelligence national objectives of education.
- Promote online life-long learning in anticipation of aging societies and technological change.
- Increase R&D funding of AI-human symbiotic evolution.
- In parallel to STEM education, create self-paced inquiry-based learning for self-actualization that increased focus on developing creativity, critical thinking, human relations, social-emotional abilities, philosophy, entrepreneurship, art, self-employment, ethics, and values (STEAM education, adding A for the Arts).
- Begin shift from mastering a profession to mastering combinations of skills.
- Teacher training schools should show how different teaching strategies affect neural activity of students' brains via fMRI and/or other means as they teach.
- Explore alternative models of education and learning (both Finland and South Korea score top in the world but have quite different systems).
- Implement insights from the Global Learning XPrize for children to teach themselves basic reading, writing, and arithmetic within 18 months.

For more information, including regional considerations in Africa, Asia, Europe, Latin America, and North America, see the Short Overview at: https://themp.org, Challenge 9, "Report" section.

Education and Learning 2030: the following graph shows the likelihood of education and learning possibilities by 2030 as judged by an International Panel of The Millennium Project. A rating of 50 on the likelihood scale would mean that there is a 50% chance the possibility will occur by 2030—in other words, that it is just as likely to occur as not to occur. An assessment of how each possibility could turn out positively and negatively as well as who will help it to occur and who might hinder it is presented in the *Education and Learning 2030* study, available in the Global Futures Intelligence System (www.themp.org), under "Research".

Figure 1.9 likelihood of education and learning possibilities by 2030

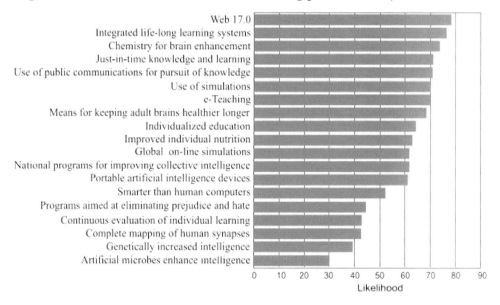

GLOBAL CHALLENGE 10. HOW CAN SHARED VALUES AND NEW SECURITY STRATEGIES REDUCE ETHNIC CONFLICTS, TERRORISM, AND THE USE OF WEAPONS OF MASS DESTRUCTION?

The vast majority of the world is living in peace. No major power wars have occurred for over 70 years; however, the nature of warfare and security has morphed today into transnational and local terrorism, international intervention into civil wars, and publicly denied cyber and information warfare. Conditions that can lead to instability exist in half the world, 65.6 million people are forcibly displaced from their homes (of whom 22.5 million are refugees today),[43] and North Korea's ICBM and thermonuclear bomb tests are condemned by the UN Security Council.

Although conflicts fell dramatically from 1990 to 2010, they have increased since then.[44] The number of armed conflicts declined slightly from 52 in 2015 to 49 in 2016,[45] and there were 14% fewer battlefield casualties in 2016 compared to 2015, and 22% fewer compared to 2014. World military spending was relatively flat from 1998 to 2011, with minor decreases 2011–14.[46] Budgets increased slightly in 2015–16, with $1.7 trillion in 2016, which is 2.2% of global gross domestic product.

According to the 2017 Global Peace Index, the world is slightly more peaceful than in the previous year; 93 countries (with 4.8 billion people) improved, while 68 deteriorated.[47] Conflict deaths fell from 167,000[48] to 157,000. However, the 2016 Global Terrorism Index[49] worsened by 6%, even

---

[43] http://www.unhcr.org/en-us/news/stories/2017/6/5941561f4/forced-displacement-worldwide-its-highest-decades.html.

[44] http://www.un.org/pga/70/wp-content/uploads/sites/10/2016/01/Conflict-and-violence-in-the-21st-century-Current-trends-as-observed-in-empirical-research-and-statistics-Mr.-Alexandre-Marc-Chief-Specialist-Fragility-Conflict-and-Violence-World-Bank-Group.pdf.

[45] https://www.prio.org/utility/DownloadFile.ashx?id=1373&type=publicationfile.

[46] https://www.sipri.org/sites/default/files/Trends-world-military-expenditure-2016.pdf.

[47] *2017 Global Peace Index*, http://visionofhumanity.org/app/uploads/2017/06/GPI17-Report.pdf.

[48] http://www.keepeek.com/Digital-Asset-Management/oecd/development/states-of-fragility-2016_9789264267213-en#.WbQ-zSiGNPY#page15.

[49] *2016 Global Terrorism Index*, http://economicsandpeace.org/wp-content/uploads/2016/11/Global-Terrorism-Index-2016.2.pdf.

though 76 countries improved while 53 deteriorated, and there was a slight reduction in deaths from terrorism. Over the past 10 years, the 2017 Fragile States Index listed 99 countries improving while 75 became more fragile, and currently it rates 34 countries between alert to very high alert for fragility.[50] OECD's States of Fragility 2016[51] reports that 50% of the world has been directly or indirectly affected by some form of political violence, there are 56 fragile contexts, 15 counties are currently extremely fragile, violence in general has increased over the past decade, and all forms of violence cost $13.6 trillion in 2015. Future effects of climate change could create up to 25 million to a billion environmental migrants by 2050,[52] which could further increase conditions for conflict.

Meanwhile, information warfare (as different than cyber warfare that attacks computers, software, and command control systems) manipulates information trusted by targets without their awareness, so that the targets will make decisions against their interest but in the interest of the one conducting information warfare. Fake news via bots, videos, and other forms of information warfare are increasingly manipulating perceptions of truth, while the public does not know how to defend itself.

Cyberattacks from governments and organized crime on other governments and corporations are expected to increase. Asymmetrical cyber warfare changes the conventional balance of power analysis. Is there a reasonable way to hold software companies accountable for hacking of their products as other businesses are responsible for failures in their products? And what scale and impact of a cyber-attack would trigger Article 5 of NATO, and what would be proportional responses? What would be the same for information warfare? U.S. intelligence services receive $53 billion[53] to bring conflicts to an end and prevent others.

---

[50] http://fundforpeace.org/fsi/2017/05/14/fsi-2017-factionalization-and-group-grievance-fuel-rise-in-instability/.
[51] http://www.oecd.org/dac/states-of-fragility-2016-9789264267213-en.htm.
[52] https://www.iom.int/migration-and-climate-change-0.
[53] https://youtu.be/aQI6sfI_d6c.

Some conflict prevention strategies include ensuring that government services are available to all groups, establishing transparent and accountable governance, holding inclusive meetings to address grievances, setting joint goals, reducing corruption, improving the free flow of information, using trade embargoes and other economic sanctions, initiating low-profile mediation, improving minority rights, controlling hate speech, providing economic aid, holding inter-religious dialogues, and using the World Court. Some conflict resolution strategies include national dialogues, international negotiations, integrating civil society actors into negotiations, military intervention, demilitarized zones, UN Peacekeeping, economic incentives, and religious leaders' initiatives. Re-war prevention strategies include reintegration of ex-combatants and displaced populations; UN Peacekeeping (especially including women in the team); truth and reconciliation commissions; rebuilding of institutions; promotion of the safe return of refugees, IDPs, and migrants; and economic development with all parties, including access to finance.

Actions to Address Global Challenge 10:

- Review the conflict resolution and prevention strategies, such as the above, as to when and why they work or fail, and teach these conclusions and integrate them into various forms of media and entertainment.
- Readjust school curricula to emphasize compassionate behavior, tolerance for diversity, peaceful resolution of conflicts, compromise, and consensus.
- Use participatory processes to produce back-casted peace scenarios to show plausible alternatives to conflict stories (see "Middle East Peace Scenarios" in Scenarios, under Research in GFIS).
- Mandate equal access of all groups to government services.
- Increase attention to ways to stop patronage and corruption.
- Integrate women into conflict reduction and peacekeeping forces.
- Conduct education programs for families and communities to detect potential terrorists and prevent them from becoming terrorists.

- Create a public online collective intelligence system to develop diplomatic, foreign policy, military, and legal systems to address the new asymmetrical threats.
- Establish NGO networks to monitor indicators of conflict and discuss and link strategies for rapid deployment of non-military resources.
- Increase use of non-lethal weapons.
- Educate people about their roles in cyber security.
- Create cyber traps and counterjamming systems to catch attackers.
- Connect early warning systems of governments and UN agencies with NGOs and the media to help generate the political will to prevent or reduce conflicts.
- Establish tracking systems of sources and destinations for weapons.
- Develop a Geneva-like Convention on cyber and information warfare.
- Implement Sustainable Development Goal 16: peace, justice, and inclusiveness.

For more information, including regional considerations, see the Short Overview at: https://themp.org, Challenge 10, "Report" section.

Figure 1.10 Terrorism incidents

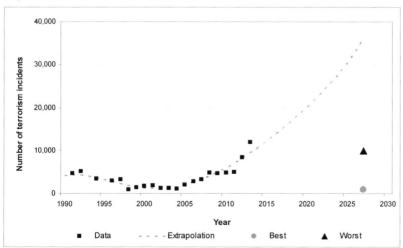

Source: Start Project, University of Maryland, with Millennium Project compilation and forecast

GLOBAL CHALLENGE 11: HOW CAN THE CHANGING STATUS OF WOMEN HELP IMPROVE THE HUMAN CONDITION?

Empowerment of women has been one of the strongest drivers of social evolution over the past century and is acknowledged as essential for addressing all the global challenges facing humanity.[54] Gender equity has entered the global consciousness and is guaranteed by the constitution of 84% of the world's nations, while "the international women's bill of rights" (CEDAW) has been ratified by all but seven[55] countries. Women's right to vote is virtually universal. Women account for 23.5%[56] of the membership of national legislative bodies, an increase from 12% in 1997, and 52 nations have had a woman head of state in the past 50 years. Nevertheless, efforts have to increase if we want to meet UN Sustainable Development Goal 5 to achieve gender equality and empower all women and girls by 2030, as more than 50% of 10-year-olds[57] live today in countries with high levels of gender inequality.

Although women contribute 52% of global work[58], their labor market participation rate[59] is only 49% compared with 76% for men and they earn up to 35% less[60] than men do. Women compose about 15% of corporate board seats worldwide, an increase of 54% since 2010.[61] Persistent discriminatory social structures have to be challenged to make progress in the future. Yet Oxfam[62] notes that if a women's paid employment rates were the same as men's, in 15 major developing economies income per capita would rise by 14% by 2020 and 20% by 2030. However, at current rate of progress, in the G20 countries it would take another 75 years[63] to achieve equal pay for equal work.

---

[54] https://www.oecd.org/dac/gender-development/47561694.pdf.

[55] http://equalmeansequal.com/international-womens-rights/.

[56] http://www.ipu.org/wmn-e/world.htm.

[57] http://www.unfpa.org/swop.

[58] http://report.hdr.undp.org/.

[59] ILO, *World Employment and Social Outlook – Trends for Women 2017.*

[60] OECD, "Pay gap," http://oecdobserver.org.

[61] http://www.catalyst.org/knowledge/women-corporate-boards-globally.

[62] https://www.oxfam.org/sites/www.oxfam.org/files/the_g20_and_gender_equality-summary_en.pdf.

[63] Ibid.

Women are more likely than men to be "solopreneurs,"[64] creating new forms of work, although lack of adequate social safety net regimes[65] put an extra burden on them. Creating equal opportunities for women would unleash creativity and foster entrepreneurship, mostly because the education gap has been generally closed and in some countries women outperform men in post-secondary education. The conversation on the status of women needs to transition from victimhood into modern-day powerhouse.

Since women drive 70–80%[66] of all consumer purchasing, and given women's educational responsibilities within the family, their education in responsible consumption could change patterns and address some of the other challenges facing humanity.

While the health gender gap is generally closing, recognizing women's reproductive rights and providing effective family planning are yet to be guaranteed around the world. Women continue to be treated as second-class citizens, and barbarian extremist practices such as female genital mutilation traumatizes millions of girls each year, with an additional 86 million potential victims[67] by 2030. Violence against women is the most under-reported crime worldwide, continuing to be perpetrated with impunity. Although 119 countries have laws that penalize domestic violence, almost 35%[68] of women experienced physical and/or sexual violence in their lifetime, and over 600 million women live in 15 countries where domestic violence is still not a crime.

Nevertheless, a Millennium Project study on changing stereotypes concluded that slow but massive shifts in gender stereotypes will occur over the next few decades. (See "Changing Gender Stereotypes" in Research section of GFIS.)

---

[64] https://www.knoll.com/knollnewsdetail/the-rise-of-co-working.

[65] European Commission, "Access to social protection for people working on non-standard contracts and as self-employed in Europe: A study of national policies 2017."

[66] Forbes, "Top 10 Things Everyone Should Know About Women Consumers," https://www.forbes.com/sites/bridgetbrennan/2015/01/21/top-10-things-everyone-should-know-about-women-consumers/

[67] UNFPA, "Let's End Female Genital Mutilation/Cutting in Our Generation," http://www.unfpa.org/press/lets-end-female-genital-mutilationcutting-our-generation.

[68] https://unstats.un.org/unsd/gender/chapter6/chapter6.html.

Actions to Address Global Challenge 11:

- Mothers should use their educational role in the family to assertively nurture gender equality and should be supported by their families, communities, and the media to do this.
- Make policies to change social structures that help women meet the demands of their careers and family responsibilities.
- Encourage girls' education, especially in STEM education and innovation to reach income parity soon.
- Where possible, ensure free (or employer-paid) preschool and child care.
- Equal remuneration for work of equal value has to be integrated into law.
- Pursue government policies that encourage female university graduates to start their own businesses.
- Occupational and sectoral segregation should be eliminated by valuing care work similarly to other professional work, thus also addressing gender stereotyping.
- Popularize mobile-phone apps that instantly report violence to police and follows up on investigation and prosecution.
- Make international aid programs conditional on respect for women's rights, enforcement of treaties protecting women rights, and prosecution.
- Apply sanctions for non-compliance on international treaties on women's rights.
- Increase women's participation in peace-building negotiations and foreign aid administration.
- Create and implement laws against treating females as second-class citizens, violence against women, patriarchal attitudes, and barbarian practices such as female genital mutilation and "honor killings."
- There should be no age limit for prosecution for violence and rape.
- Ensure a woman's rights to land ownership and financing.

- Fight gender stereotyping in the media and increase the percent of women executives in journalism.
- Add martial arts and other forms of self-defence in elementary and secondary schools' physical education classes for girls, not only for self-defence but also as a deterrence policy.

For more information, including regional considerations in Africa, Asia, Europe, Latin America, and North America, see the Short Overview at: https://themp.org, Challenge 11, "Report" section.

Figure 1.11 Proportion of seats held by women in national parliaments (% of members)

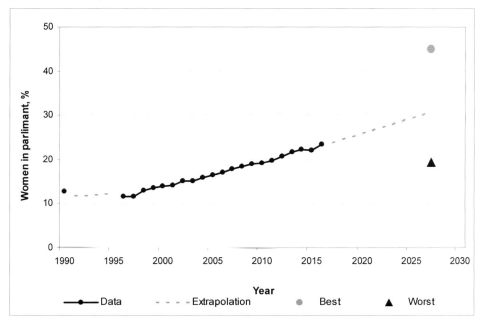

Source: IPU, with Millennium Project compilation and forecast

GLOBAL CHALLENGE 12: HOW CAN TRANSNATIONAL ORGANIZED CRIME NETWORKS BE STOPPED FROM BECOMING MORE POWERFUL AND SOPHISTICATED GLOBAL ENTERPRISES?

Organized crime takes in over $3 trillion per year, which is twice all military annual budgets combined. Havocscope.com estimates the value of black market trade in 50 categories from 91 countries (105 countries not included) at $1.81 trillion,[69] not including extortion, racketeering, corruption, and money laundering (due to their overlapping nature). Cybercrimes are also not included, but businesses may lose $2 trillion due to cybercrime in 2019.[70] Moreover, governments, lobbyists, and organized crime networks are increasingly suspected of information and cyberwarfare collusion to affect national elections.[71] Distinctions among organized crime, insurgency, and terrorism have begun to blur, giving new markets for organized crime and increasing threats to democracies, development, and security.

In addition to these financial implications, the human misery of terrorized villagers caught in gang wars to deaths around the world due to fake drugs are truly a crime against humanity that the ICC does not yet recognize. For example, WHO estimates 50% of all medication purchased online is fake, resulting in an estimated $200 billion income to crime per year, not including the hundreds of thousands of deaths that result affecting families and development. Offline transfers are also growing: 900 million[72] counterfeit and illicit medicines were seized at the borders in Africa in 2016.

Although the UN Convention against Transnational Organized Crime came into force in 2003, a global prosecution strategy has not emerged. OECD's Financial Action Task Force has made 40 good recommendations to counter money laundering, and the Council of Europe's Convention on

---

[69] http://www.havocscope.com/.
[70] https://www.forbes.com/sites/stevemorgan/2016/01/17/cyber-crime-costs-projected-to-reach-2-trillion-by-2019/#5365bae13a91.
[71] https://www.apnews.com/2512bac1ad6b4ea08c0b2388db0454d2.
[72] http://www.iracm.com/en/2017/01/new-record-seizures-illicit-medicines-africa-counterfeit-medicines-africa-time-assessment-2/.

Laundering came into force in May 2008, but the impacts are not clear. After years of Millennium Project interviews of relevant senior government officials, the outlines of a global strategy to counter TOC has emerged.

A financial prosecution system could be established as a new body to complement the related organizations addressing various parts of TOC today. In cooperation with these organizations, the new system would identify and establish priorities on top criminal groups (defined by the amount of money laundered) to be prosecuted one at a time. It would prepare legal cases, identify suspects' assets that can be frozen, establish the current location of the suspects, assess the local authorities' ability to make an arrest, and send the case to one of a number of preselected courts. Such courts, like UN peacekeeping forces, could be established and trained, and then be ready for instant duty. When investigations are complete, arrest orders would be executed to apprehend the criminal(s), freeze access to their assets, open the court case, and then proceed to the next TOC group or individual on the priority list. Prosecution would be outside the country of the accused. Although extradition is accepted by the UN Convention against Transnational Organized Crime, a new protocol would be necessary for courts to be deputized, similar to the way military forces are deputized for UN peacekeeping. Each time a court would be needed, it could be selected via a lottery system among volunteering countries. After initial government funding, the system would receive its financial support from frozen assets of convicted criminals rather than depending on government contributions, which could be subject to bribery by organized crime. Countries that made the arrests and courts that prosecuted the cases would receive reimbursements from the frozen assets.

Actions to Address Global Challenge 12:
- Conduct a feasibility study of the above strategy.
- Include organized crime as a crime against humanity recognized by the ICC.

- Study transferability of India's demonetization reduction of organized crime.
- Draw lessons from Colombia's defeat of the FARC, which sustained its armed insurgency with illicit drug trafficking, illegal mining, and extortion.
- Engage farmers in high-income agricultural alternatives to illegal production.

For more information, including regional considerations in Africa, Asia, Europe, Latin America, and North America, see the Short Overview at: https://themp.org, Challenge 12, "Report" section.

GLOBAL CHALLENGE 13: HOW CAN GROWING ENERGY DEMANDS BE MET SAFELY AND EFFICIENTLY?

The Paris Agreement is expected to reduce fossil fuel consumption and increase renewable sources of energy. Solar and wind energy are cost-completive with coal (especially when the cost externalities are considered), and massive lithium-ion battery production plants are in construction to help renewables' ability to provide baseload electricity. Renewable power generation added a record 138.5GW or 55.3% of all new power generation in 2016. According to the OECD, nearly 70% of planned additions to the power capacity in G20 countries are for renewable sources, compared with 22% from coal. In 2015 China past Germany to become the biggest producer of solar energy, and it plans to invest 2.5 trillion yuan ($361 billion) in renewable power generation between 2016 and 2020.

Coal saw a dramatic reduction in 2016. The amount of coal power capacity in pre-construction planning fell 48%, from 1,090 GW in January 2016 to 570 GW in January 2017.[73] In 2016, 13 provinces in China were ordered to halt new approvals of coal plants due to capacity redundancy, resulting in an 85% drop in new permits. Furthermore, 15 provinces were ordered to halt construction of already approved coal plants.[74] In China and India, 68 GW of construction is now frozen at over 100 project sites. Worldwide, more construction is now frozen than entered construction in the past year. Coal plant closings are taking place at an unprecedented pace, with 64 GW of retirements in the past two years, mainly in the European Union and the United States.

The price of fossil fuels does not include what governments pay to address health costs, environmental damages, and other externalities from the fossil fuel industries; when included, the IMF estimates that the fossil fuel industries receive $5.3 trillion[75] in subsidies per year. And the world still

---

[73] *Boom and Bust 2017: Tracking the Global Coal Plan Pipeline,*
http://endcoal.org/wp-content/uploads/2017/03/BoomBust2017-English-Final.pdf.
[74] https://www.chinadialogue.net/blog/9587-2-17-set-to-be-a-bleak-year-for-coal-/en.
[75] https://www.imf.org/en/News/Articles/2015/09/28/04/53/sonew070215a.

depends on fossil sources for 80% of its primary energy. Nuclear power produces about 10% of the world's electricity, with 449 plants[76] in 30 countries,[77] of which nearly 60% are past their 30-year lifetime and store their nuclear waste onsite. About 50 plants are in some stage of decommissioning and only 17 plants have ever been fully decommissioned. Hackers have begun penetrating nuclear power companies' computer networks, rising security questions. Nevertheless, about 60 plants are under construction in 15 countries.

The future of oil is also in question, with advances in electric self-driving and plug-in hybrid cars and cars that run on hydrogen and natural gas. Energy companies are racing to make enough safe energy by 2050 for an additional 3.4 billion people (1.2 billion who do not have access now, plus 2.2 billion in population[78] growth). The 100% renewable energy movement is rapidly emerging around the world.[79] Interesting ideas in R&D include spay-on solar cells for windows, making skyscrapers net energy producers; small batteries recharged by body heat and motion; retrofitting coal plants for CO_2 capture and reuse; solar panel roads and roof tiles; AI to dramatically improve efficiency (of the electric grid, IoT, transportation, etc.); producing hydrogen from plants instead of CO_2 via synthetic biology; solar farms focused on Stirling engines; high-altitude (500–2000 meters) wind energy; drilled hot rock enhanced geothermal systems; and energy storage systems from liquid air.[80] Longer-range options that could supply abundant GHG-free energy for all, such as hot and/or cold fusion and solar power satellites to beam energy anywhere on Earth or near-space, are being pursued.

---

[76] https://www.nei.org/Knowledge-Center/Nuclear-Statistics/World-Statistics.
[77] If Taiwan is counted as a country, then it would be 31 and the number under construction would be 16.
[78] UN *World Population Prospects: The 2017 Revision*, https://www.un.org/development/desa/en/news/population/world-population-prospects-2017.html.
[79] http://www.go100re.net/.
[80] http://www.renewableenergyworld.com/articles/print/volume-19/issue-4/features/energy-storage/a-look-at-liquid-air-energy-storage-technology.html.

Actions to Address Global Challenge 13:

- Commit to a US-China Apollo-like 10-year energy goal with a NASA-like R&D system to achieve it (if the U.S. falters, then a China-EU-India goal).
- Increase subsidies for renewables and reduce subsidies for fossil fuels.
- Periodically publicize country progress on the Paris Agreement.
- Increase investments into interesting ideas in R&D listed above.
- Work with International Renewable Energy Agency to harmonize regulations and standards for more predictable investment conditions.
- Establish a globally accessible collective intelligence system for energy.

For more information, including regional considerations in Africa, Asia, Europe, Latin America, and North America, see the Short Overview at: https://themp.org, Challenge 13, "Report" section.

Figure 1.12 Electricity production from renewable sources, excluding hydroelectric (% of total)

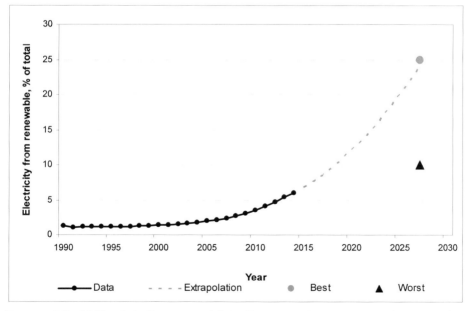

Source: World Bank indicators, with Millennium Project compilation and forecast

GLOBAL CHALLENGE 14: HOW CAN SCIENTIFIC AND TECHNOLOGICAL BREAKTHROUGHS BE ACCELERATED TO IMPROVE THE HUMAN CONDITION?

The speed of scientific breakthroughs and technological applications to improve the human condition is being accelerated by computational science and engineering, artificial intelligence, common database protocols, Moore's law, and Nielsen's law of internet bandwidth (50% speed increase per year).[81] Future synergies among synthetic biology, 3D/4D printing, artificial intelligence, robotics, atomically precise fabrication and other forms of nanotechnology, tele-everything, drones, augmented and virtual reality, falling costs of renewable energy systems, and collective intelligence systems will make the last 25 years seem slow compared with the next 25.

China has demonstrated quantum entanglement between an orbital satellite and Earth and is creating a quantum communications network between Beijing and Shanghai. The HP Laser Fusion 3D printer can print 30 million voxels (3D pixels) per second. Hyperloop feasibility studies are under way in Czechia, France, Indonesia, Slovakia, UAE, and the U.S.[82] IBM's Watson already diagnoses cancer better than doctors, robots learn to walk faster than toddlers, and Google's AlphaGo beat the champion Go player. China is expected to have nearly 40%[83] of all robots in the world by 2019, up from 27% in 2015.

International R&D spending is forecast to be 1.71% of global GDP in 2017, while the U.S. and South Korea forecast 2.83% and 4.29% of their GDP respectively. WIPO received 233,000[84] international patent applications in 2016, a 7% increase from 2015, led by the U.S., Japan, China (which increased 44%), and Germany.

---

[81] http://www.huawei.com/us/publications/communicate/78/single-wavelength-for-100g-access-en.
[82] http://www.reuters.com/article/us-usa-hyperloop/high-speed-hyperloop-project-ready-for-key-test-in-nevada-idUSKBN19Y2XZ?utm_source=applenews.
[83] https://ifr.org/news/ifr-press-release/deployment-of-robots-soars-70-percent-in-asia-846/.
[84] http://www.wipo.int/pressroom/en/articles/2017/article_0002.html

As of June 2017, China's TaihuLight (93 petaflops) and Tianhe-2 (33.9 petaflops) are the two fastest computers,[85] followed by Switzerland's Piz Daint (19.6 petaflops). The U.S. has the next three fastest computers. However, Japan may pass all with a new 130 petaflops[86] computer quite soon, and the U.S. has just added more funds into supercomputer development. Meanwhile D-Wave, the quantum computer systems and software company in Canada, is exploring the coverage of quantum computing[87] and machine learning to create quantum AI.[88] Data storage in single molecules promises to increase data storage density by factors of 100.[89] By 2050 everyone could have access to cloud quantum/AI anywhere at any time for nearly anything to help experience the best use of one's time each moment.

However, this also means that everything is potentially vulnerable—from hacking driverless cars, planes, and ships to brain/computer interfaces and nanomedicine. Synthetic biology inventions could escape their environments, causing massive damage to nature. Solutions to the nanotech "gray goo" problem (endless self-replicating nano machines) are not yet convincing. Future artificial general intelligence could evolve beyond human control and understanding. Some science/philosophers think that AI is a natural next step in evolution.[90]

E-waste pollution is growing worldwide, with the potential to poison groundwater. Nanoparticles might bio-accumulate in the body, causing

---

[85] https://www.top500.org/lists/2017/06/.

[86] http://www.pcworld.com/article/3144541/cloud-computing/japan-plans-superefficient-supercomputer-by-2017.html.

[87] https://www.nature.com/articles/ncomms15971.

[88] https://www.dwavesys.com/press-releases/d-wave-joins-creative-destruction-lab-foster-startups-quantum-machine-learning.

[89] http://www.kurzweilai.net/single-molecule-level-data-storage-may-achieve-100-times-higher-data-density?utm_source=KurzweilAI+Weekly+Newsletter&utm_campaign=9a2f209cbd-UA-946742-1&utm_medium=email&utm_term=0_147a5a48c1-9a2f209cbd-282100129.

[90] Max Tegmark, "Life 3.0: Being Human In The Age Of Artificial Intelligence, 2017," http://www.kurzweilai.net/will-ai-enable-the-third-stage-of-life?utm_source=KurzweilAI+Weekly+Newsletter&utm_campaign=9a2f209cbd-UA-946742-1&utm_medium=email&utm_term=0_147a5a48c1-9a2f209cbd-282100129.

health problems. The industrial and information ages produced more jobs than they eliminated; but the speed, capacity, synergies, scope, and global dynamics of the coming technological changes may make it different this time. The sooner the world has serious and systematic conversations about these issues, the more likely the acceleration of S&T can benefit humanity. (See Chapter 4 on Future Work/Technology 2050.)

In the meantime, computer-mediated elementary brain-to-brain communications have been demonstrated; autonomous (and semi-autonomous) robots have conducted surgery; AI has been used to erase painful memories; experiments with gene editing of gamete cells and human embryos have the potential for eliminating inherited diseases and tendencies to get other diseases;[91] stem cells are being used to repair tissue, potentially altering the aging process; and genetic code has been transmitted in digital form to print viruses,[92] demonstrating the ability to teleport life forms to remote locations, even distant planets.

Norway is ready to launch the first robot battery-powered crewless cargo ship,[93] massive artificial photosynthesis[94] is in development for new forms of energy and materials and to absorb atmospheric CO_2 more efficiently than nature to help reverse climate change, and NASA's Kepler telescope has detected nearly 1,300 exoplanets, upping the odds of future contact with extraterrestrial life.

So, what else is next? New combinations and manipulations of genetic molecules and life forms will be developed to create the biological revolution, as new combinations of matter and energy created the industrial revolution. Atomically precise fabrication will build machines to revolutionize efficiency of physical production. Implantable biosensors in micro-robots in the body will diagnose and provide therapies while transmitting virtual reality imagery outside the body. Space elevators between Earth and orbit may give low-cost

---

[91] https://www.nature.com/nature/journal/v548/n7668/full/nature23305.html.
[92] https://www.technologyreview.com/s/608388/biological-teleporter-could-seed-life-through-galaxy/.
[93] https://www.theverge.com/2017/7/24/16018652/first-autonomous-ship-launch-2018.
[94] http://solarfuelshub.org/who-we-are/overview.

access to space, and longer-range options for space travel[95] are being explored, such as matter-antimatter reactions, fusion, ion drive, photonic propulsion, plasma ejection, and solar sails. However, over 750,000 pieces of debris (one centimeter in diameter or more) travelling at 27,400 kilometers per hour (17,000 mrh) are orbiting Earth, threatening future access to outer space.

There is little relationship between some of the accelerating advances in S&T and what is covered in the conventional news, discussed by politicians, taught in schools, or filling the public mind around the world. The history of S&T demonstrates that advances can have unintended negative consequences as well as benefits. We need a global collective intelligence system to track S&T advances, forecast consequences, and document a range of views so that all can understand the potential consequences of new and possible future S&T and from this develop policies that create incentives for S&T to address our global challenges.

As a result of all these changes, and others not yet on the horizon, far more individuals will have far more access to far more powerful means to access more capacities worldwide at far lower costs with far less control by power elites than in the past.

Actions to Address Global Challenge 14:
- Create global means to link research agendas to human needs and threats.
- Establish some kind of international S&T organization to improve the human condition more as an online public access global collective intelligence system rather than as an intergovernmental body like UNESCO.
- Support research to prevent future artificial super intelligence evolving against human interests.
- Encourage scientist to take an oath similar to the Hippocratic Oath taken by physicians to "do no harm."

---

[95] http://wallstreetpit.com/112890-interstellar-travel-possible/.

- Pass laws to prosecute "patent trolls" (firms that don't produce anything but simply file patent lawsuits for extortion) to drop deceitful patent law cases.
- Create systems to remove space debris, or else access to space may become too hazardous.
- Explore ways to limit access to materials and S&T information that can be used by individuals for destructive purposes.

For more information, including regional considerations in Africa, Asia, Europe, Latin America, and North America, see the Short Overview at: https://themp.org, Challenge 14, "Report" section.

Figure1.13 R&D expenditures (% of GDP)

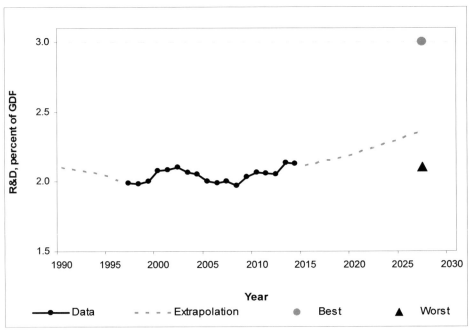

Source: World Bank indicators, with Millennium Project compilation and forecast

GLOBAL CHALLENGE 15: HOW CAN ETHICAL CONSIDERATIONS BECOME MORE ROUTINELY INCORPORATED INTO GLOBAL DECISIONS?

Increasingly, decisions are being made by AI; since their algorithms are not ethically neutral, the future of ethics will in part be influenced by auditing ethical assumptions in software. It will also be influenced by the flood of new information channels that are used to pollute and distort perceptions, leading many to rethink how to know the truth of global developments. Information warfare has been waged against national elections. Political spin masters drown out the pursuit of truth. We need to learn how to prevent or counter information warfare and fake news.

At the same time, an increasingly educated and Internet-connected generation is increasingly rising up against the abuse of power and demanding accountability. The release of the Panama Papers in April 2016 exposed corruption worldwide. Surveillance implications of the IoT connected with AI could deter unethical decisionmaking. New technologies also make it easier for more people to do more good at a faster pace than ever before. The rising number of protests around the world shows a growing unwillingness to tolerate unethical decisionmaking by power elites.

Although short-term economic "me-first" attitudes are prevalent throughout the world, love for humanity, solidarity, and global consciousness are also evident in the norms expressed in the many transnational political movements, inter-religious dialogues, UN organizations, international philanthropy, the Olympic spirit, refugee relief, development programs for poorer nations, NGOs like Doctors Without Borders, and international journalism. Global ethics are emerging around the world through the evolution of ISO standards and international treaties that are defining the norms of civilization. The Universal Declaration of Human Rights continues to shape discussions about global ethics and justice and to influence decisions across ethical, religious, and ideological divides. The International Criminal Court has indicted over 40 leaders, and the World Court has delivered 126 judgments between nation-states. Corporate social responsibility programs, ethical marketing, and social investing are increasing. The UN Global Compact is reinforcing ethics in business decisionmaking.

However, corporate behavior can be less ethical in lower-income countries—for example, waste disposal and cigarette advertising. Corporate advanced marketing methods that bypass consumers' deliberative capacities based on cognitive and behavioral sciences raise new questions of ethics. Transparency International's 2016 Corruption Perceptions Index[96] shows deterioration over the past several years; it found that over two-thirds of the 176 countries and territories assessed scored below 50 (on a scale from 0=highly corrupt to 100=very clean). The Global Slavery Index estimates that 45.8 million[97] people were in some form of modern slavery in 2016 in 167 countries assessed and that 58% are in five countries (India, China, Pakistan, Bangladesh, and Uzbekistan); as a percent of population, however, the highest numbers are found in North Korea, Uzbekistan, Cambodia, India, and Qatar. Press freedom has been decreasing over the decade,[98] and the global concentration of wealth has become obscene.[99] The proliferation of unethical decisions that led to the 2008 financial crisis and 2009 global recession clearly demonstrate the interdependence of economic results and ethics.

The moral will to act in collaboration across national, institutional, political, religious, and ideological boundaries that is necessary to address today's global challenges requires global ethics. Public morality based on religious metaphysics is challenged daily by growing secularism, leaving many unsure about the moral basis for decisionmaking. Many turn back to old traditions for guidance, giving rise to fundamentalist movements in many religions today. Unfortunately, religions and ideologies that claim moral

---

[96] https://www.transparency.org/news/feature/corruption_perceptions_index_2016.
[97] https://www.globalslaveryindex.org/findings/.
[98] *2017 World Press Freedom Index*, https://rsf.org/en/2017-world-press-freedom-index-tipping-point.
[99] "Just eight men own the same wealth as half the world," https://www.oxfam.org/en/pressroom/pressreleases/2017-01-16/just-8-men-own-same-wealth-half-world.

superiority give rise to "we-they" splits that are being played out in conflicts around the world.

The acceleration of scientific and technological change seems to be beyond conventional means of ethical evaluation. Is it ethical to clone ourselves or bring dinosaurs back to life or to invent thousands of new life forms through synthetic biology? Since there is little time to assess daily S&T advances, is it time to invent anticipatory ethical systems? Just as law has a body of previous judgments to draw on for guidance, will we also need bodies of ethical judgments about possible future events? For example, in the foreseeable future it may be possible for individuals acting alone to make and deploy weapons of mass destruction. To prevent this possibility, will governments sacrifice citizen privacy? Will families and communities be more effective in nurturing more mentally healthy, moral people? Will public health and education systems create early detection and intervention strategies? The consequences of the failure to raise moral, mentally healthy people will be more serious in the future than in the past. Technologies accessible to individuals, organizations, and governments have become too powerful and diverse to allow the growth of unethical behavior.

Actions to Address Global Challenge 15:
- Create audit procedures to expose ethical assumptions in algorithms.
- Establish an international IAEA-like system to deter cyber and information warfare.
- Enforce measures to reduce corruption such as those recommended by Transparency International.
- Require civics and ethics in all forms of education, focusing on making behavior match the values people say they believe in.
- Promote parental guidance to establish a sense of values.
- Make ethics part of performance evaluation criteria.
- Develop new social contracts between governments and citizens' rights and responsibilities to prevent future forms of massively destructive terrorism.

- Explore how transparency policies can be implemented.
- Use entertainment media to promote memes like "make decisions that are good for me, you, and the world."
- Revoke corrupt officials' travel visas.
- Create better incentives for ethics in global decisions.

For more information, including regional considerations in Africa, Asia, Europe, Latin America, and North America, see the Short Overview at: https://themp.org, Challenge 15, "Report" section.

Figure1.14 CPIA transparency, accountability, and corruption in the public sector rating (1=low; 6=high)

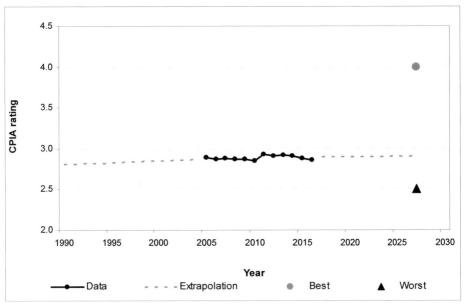

Source: World Bank indicators, with Millennium Project compilation and forecast

*   *   *

Your feedback is invited to help improve the overview of these 15 global challenges for future print and downloadable editions, as well as online in GFIS, at https://themp.org. Please email us at <info@millennium-project.org> or subscribe to the Global Futures Intelligence System at www.themp.org to participate in the full system.

Figure 1.15 is a graphic representation of The Millennium Project's process on identifying and updating the Global Challenges and the development of the State of the Future Index.

Figure 1.15 Global Challenges and SOFI Process

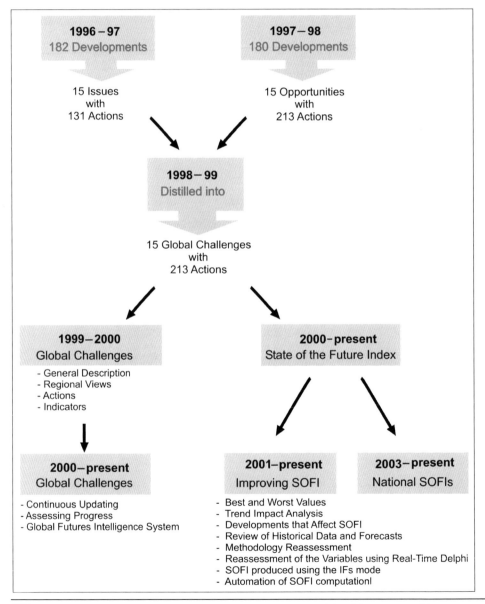

2.

STATE OF THE FUTURE INDEX

Assessing the impact and the interplay of the different potential developments affecting the future is a difficult and controversial task, but it is nevertheless valuable and necessary for coherent policymaking. Quantitative assessment of the factors of change helps us understand the system and supports the setting of priorities.

The State of the Future Index is an indication of the 10-year outlook for the future based on 20 years of historical data for a selected group of variables that in combination can depict potential systemic change. It is constructed with key indicators that are individually forecast and then aggregated to indicate the potential direction and intensity of change. It shows a potential trend; it is not a projection. Its role is solely to help understand the system and the relationships among its items—how changes to individual or several variables ripple throughout the system.

Combining many variables into a single index can lead to loss of detail, hide certain aspects by compensating losses in some areas with progress in the others, and mask variations among sectors, regions, or nations. The apparent precision of an index should not be mistaken for accuracy.

Nevertheless, the SOFI can be useful for assessing the consequences of different policies and for showing the combined potential outcomes in an easy-to-understand fashion. It has been produced by The Millennium Project since 2000. For the methodology, see "State of the Future Index" in the Futures Research Methodology section of GFIS (http.themp.org).

The variables included in the SOFI, as well as their respective weights (importance to the system) and the "best" and "worst" values in the next decade have been decided through RTD studies and updated by The Millennium Project staff. The sources of data have been carefully considered, are deemed to be reliable, and have good historical data records.

SOFI is in continuous evolution and adapted to global changes. Box 2.1 presents the variables included in the computation of the 2017 SOFI. The most important changes to the computation of the 2017 SOFI compared with earlier SOFIs include:

New variables were added and some variables were replaced with new ones (e.g., "Social unrest indicator" has been added; "Fossil fuel and cement production emissions" has been replaced with "CO_2-equivalent mixing ratio (ppm)").

Historical data were updated, and new series were inserted when old series were discontinued.

New curve fit equations were derived, and new interpolations were made for missing data.

The baseline SOFI that resulted from the use of the new data sets for the variables is shown in Figure 2.1. The data and their sources, extrapolations, and equations for forecasting are available in the State of the Future Index section in GFIS (http://themp.org) under "Research."

Box 2.1 Variables included in the computation of 2017 SOFI

1. GNI per capita, PPP (constant 2011 international $) (world)
2. Economic income inequality (income share held by highest 10%)
3. Unemployment, total (% of world labor force)
4. Poverty headcount ratio at $1.90 a day (2011 PPP) (% of population)
5. CPIA transparency, accountability, and corruption in the public sector rating (1=low; 6=high)
6. Foreign direct investment, net inflows (BoP, current $, billions)
7. R&D expenditures (% of GDP) (world)
8. Population growth (annual %)
9. Life expectancy at birth (years)
10. Mortality rate, infant (per 1,000 live births)
11. Prevalence of undernourishment (% of population)
12. Health expenditure per capita (current $)
13. Physicians (per 1,000 people)
14. Improved water source (% of population with access)
15. Renewable internal freshwater resources per capita (cubic meters)
16. Biocapacity per capita (gha)
17. Forest area (% of land area)
18. CO_2-equivalent mixing ratio (ppm)
19. Energy efficiency (GDP per unit of energy use)
20. Electricity production from renewable sources, excl. hydro (% of total)
21. Literacy rate, adult total (% of people aged 15 and above)
22. School enrollment, secondary (% gross)
23. Share of high-skilled employment (%)
24. Number of wars and armed conflicts
25. Terrorism incidents
26. Social unrest indicator (number of protest events/ total events) (%)
27. Freedom rights (number of countries rated "free")
28. Proportion of seats held by women in national parliaments (%)
29. Internet users (per 100 people)

Figure 2.1 State of the Future Index 2017

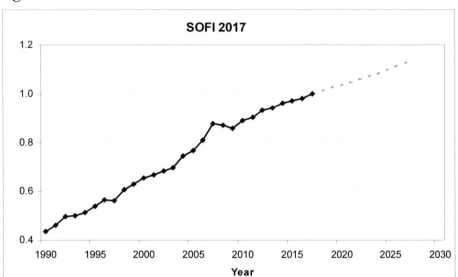

A one-to-one comparison with the SOFIs prepared in earlier years would be misleading, since some of the variables have changed. Overall, however, the shape of this year's SOFI is similar to earlier ones. The growth rate for the coming decade will be 1.14%, considerably slower than 3.14% for the period 1990–2017. This is mostly due to the slow recovery after the 2008 economic turmoil and because many of the hindering factors are aggravating problems. For instance, one of the variables that has a large impact on the 2017 SOFI projection is the number of terrorist attacks, which is highly unknowable. If terrorism could be contained, the world's outlook and the rate of growth would appear to be considerably better.

SOFI can be used to test the potential impact of various policies on the entire system. As an example, the graph in Figure 2.2 indicates the potential impact of improving two variables by 2027: reducing by 15% GHG emissions (in CO_2-equivalent) and a combined effect by adding to it a 15% reduction of income inequality.

A sensitivity analysis shows that other variables with relatively significant potential impact on the overall SOFI are electricity production from renewable sources and energy efficiency (GDP per unit of energy use).

One of the advantages of computing the SOFI is the identification of the areas where we are winning, losing, or stagnating—thereby helping set priorities. Figures 2.3 and 2.4 show where humanity is making progress and where more political attention and efforts are needed. This can be further analyzed by assessing the individual variables and their potential trajectories. (Figures 2.6 to 2.34 at the end of this section show the graphs of the individual variables with their respective extrapolations.)

The world seems to be making progress in more areas than it is regressing or stagnating in, but since the areas of stagnation or regress are crucially important for human and planetary survival, addressing them should be a top priority.

Figure 2.2 State of the Future Index 2017 with sensitivity analysis

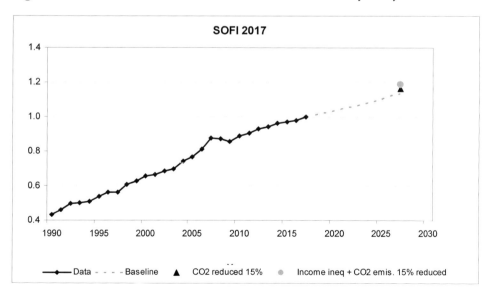

Figure 2.3 Where we are winning

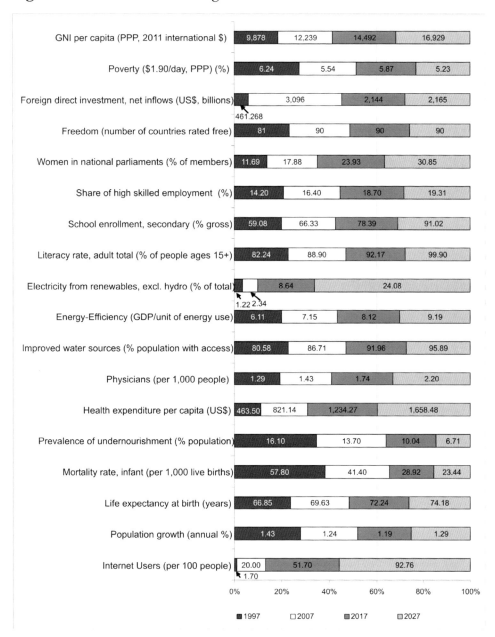

Figure 2.4 Where we are losing or there is no progress

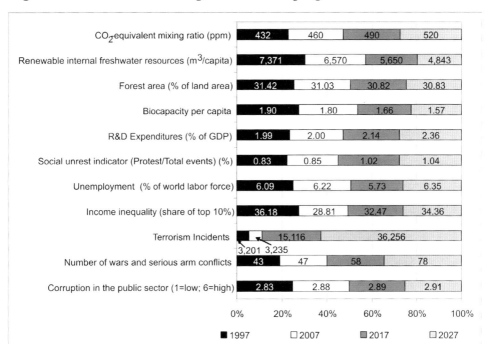

NATIONAL SOFI

SOFI can be—and has been—computed for nation-states. SOFIs could also be constructed for different domains (e.g., a SOFI for artificial intelligence or a SOFI for the knowledge economy). The national SOFIs that have been computed over the years are available in the State of the Future Index section in GFIS, under "Research." This year, the featured national SOFI is that computed by Pakistan. The set of variables included in the Pakistan 2017 SOFI is presented in Box 2.2, while Figure 2.5 shows the graph.

Box 2.2 Variables included in the Pakistan SOFI 2017

1. Population, total
2. CO_2 emissions (kt)
3. Energy produced from non-fission, non-fossil sources (% of total primary national energy supply)
4. Food production index
5. Forestlands (% of national land area)
6. Freedom level
7. GDP per capita (constant 2010 US$)
8. GDP per unit of energy use (constant 2011 PPP $ per kg of oil equivalent)
9. Intentional homicides (per 100,000 people)
10. Mortality rate, infant (per 1,000 live births)
11. Internet users (% of population)
12. CPIA transparency, accountability, and corruption in the public sector
13. Life expectancy at birth, total (years)
14. Youth literacy rate, population 15-24 years, both sexes (%)
15. Percent of refugees displaced from and within the country
16. People killed in terrorist attacks
17. People voting in elections (% of national population of voting age)
18. Physicians (per 10,000 people)
19. Population growth (annual %)
20. Improved water source (% of population with access)
21. Poverty headcount ratio at $1.90 a day (2011 PPP) (% of population)
22. Malaria—number of cases confirmed with microscopy
23. Research and development expenditure (% of GDP)
24. Tertiary education (University)
25. Seats held by women in national parliament (% of members)
26. Total debt service (percent of GNI)
27. Unemployment, total (% of total national labor force)
28. Imports (million $)
29. Exports (million $)
30. Federal taxes (total) (million $)
31. Inflation, consumer prices (annual %)

Figure 2.5 Pakistan SOFI 2017

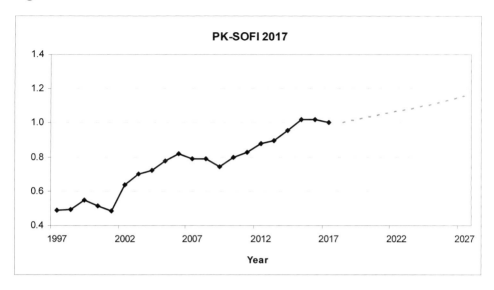

SOFI's computation at global, national, and regional or sectoral levels is being continuously improved in methodology, set of variables, and computation technique. The Millennium Project is also working on developing an automated computation, to make it easier for anyone to construct SOFIs tailored to their specific objectives.

VARIABLES INCLUDED IN THE GLOBAL 2017 SOFI

For the 10-year estimates, the best fit curve has been selected, using the CurveExpert Professional software. Hence, they are mathematical extrapolations and cannot be considered projections or professional forecasts.

Figure 2.6 GNI per capita, PPP (constant 2011 international $)

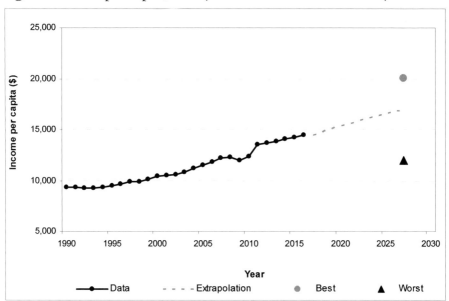

Source: World Bank indicators, with Millennium Project compilation and forecast

Figure 2.7 Economic income inequality (Income share held by highest 10%)

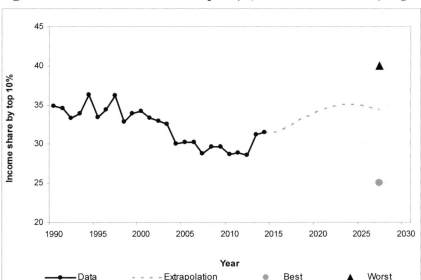

Source: World Bank indicators, with Millennium Project compilation and forecast

Figure 2.8 Unemployment, total (% of world labor force)

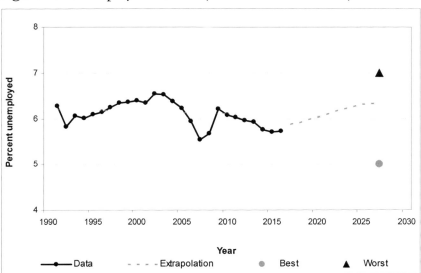

Source: ILO 2017 global report, with Millennium Project compilation and forecast

Figure 2.9 Poverty headcount ratio at $1.90 a day (2011 PPP) (% of population)

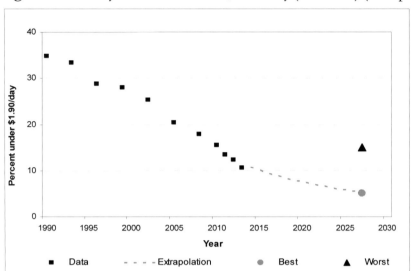

Source: World Bank indicators, with Millennium Project compilation and forecast

Figure 2.10 CPIA transparency, accountability, and corruption in the public sector rating (1=low; 6=high)

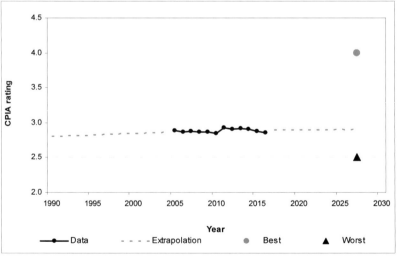

Source: World Bank indicators, with Millennium Project compilation and forecast

Figure 2.11 Foreign direct investment, net inflows (BoP, current $, billions)

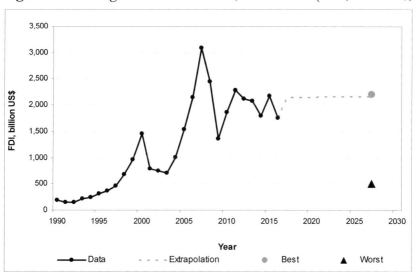

Source: World Bank indicators, with Millennium Project compilation and forecast

Figure 2.12 R&D expenditures (% of GDP)

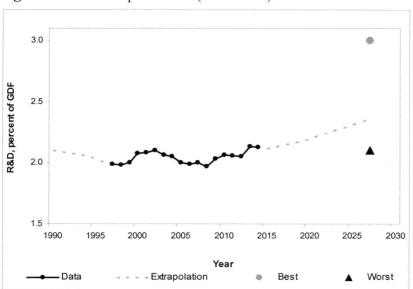

Source: World Bank indicators, with Millennium Project compilation and forecast

Figure 2.13 Population growth (annual %)

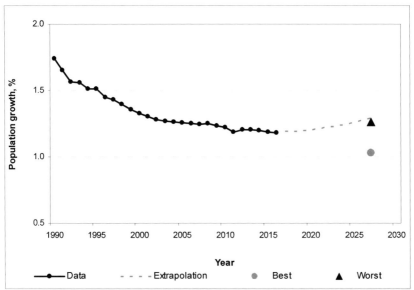

Source: World Bank indicators, with Millennium Project compilation and forecast

Figure 2.14 Life expectancy at birth (years)

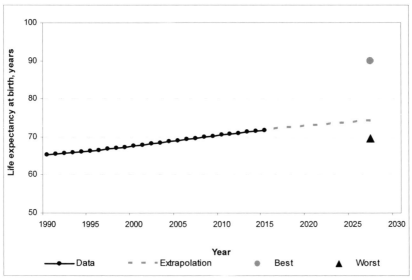

Source: World Bank indicators, with Millennium Project compilation and forecast

Figure 2.15 Mortality rate, infant (per 1,000 live births)

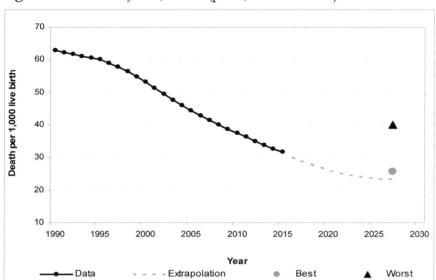

Source: World Bank indicators, with Millennium Project compilation and forecast

Figure 2.16 Prevalence of undernourishment (% of population)

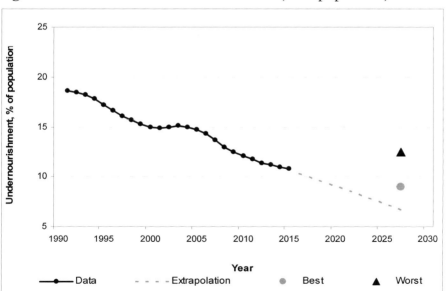

Source: World Bank indicators, with Millennium Project compilation and forecast

Figure 2.17 Health expenditure per capita (current $)

Source: World Bank indicators, with Millennium Project compilation and forecast

Figure 2.18 Physicians (per 1,000 people)

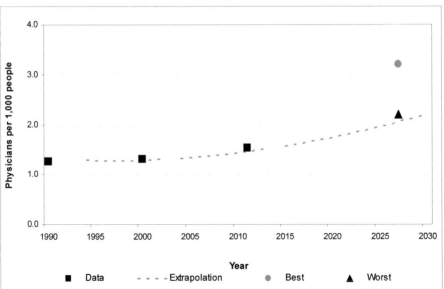

Source: World Bank indicators, with Millennium Project compilation and forecast

Figure 2.19 Improved water sources (% of population with access)

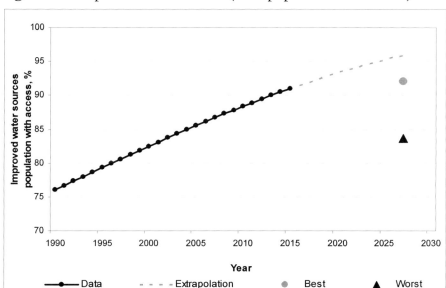

Source: World Bank indicators, with Millennium Project compilation and forecast

Figure 2.20 Renewable internal freshwater resources per capita (cubic meters)

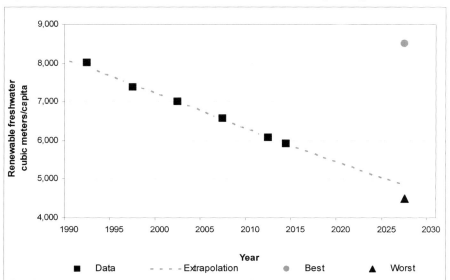

Source: World Bank indicators, with Millennium Project compilation and forecast

Figure 2.21 Biocapacity per capita (gha)

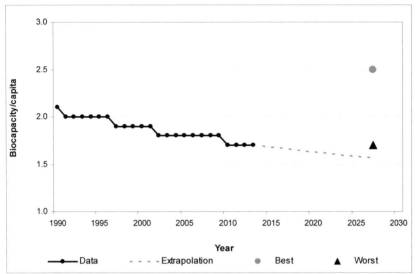

Source: Global Footprint Network, with Millennium Project compilation and forecast

Figure 2.22 Forest area (% of land area)

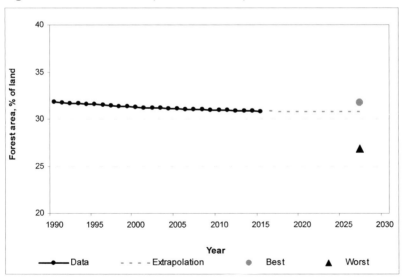

Source: World Bank indicators, with Millennium Project compilation and forecast

Figure 2.23 GHG emissions, CO_2-equivalent mixing ratio (ppm)

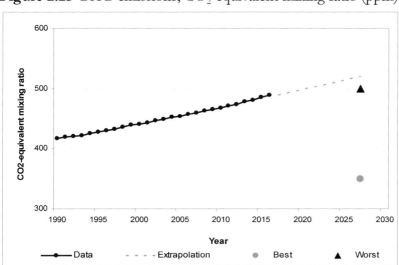

Source: NOAA Earth System Research Laboratory, with Millennium Project compilation and forecast

Figure 2.24 Energy efficiency (GDP per unit of energy use (constant 2011 PPP $ per kg of oil equivalent))

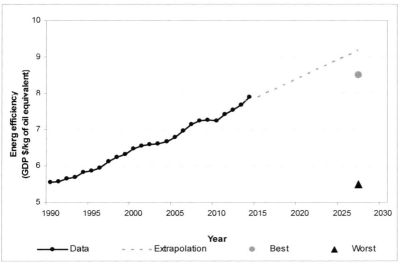

Source: World Bank indicators, with Millennium Project compilation and forecast

Figure 2.25 Electricity production from renewable sources, excluding hydroelectric (% of total)

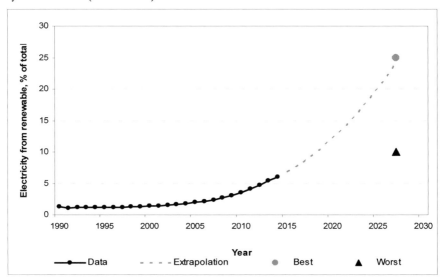

Source: World Bank indicators, with Millennium Project compilation and forecast

Figure 2.26 Literacy rate, adult total (% of people aged 15 and above)

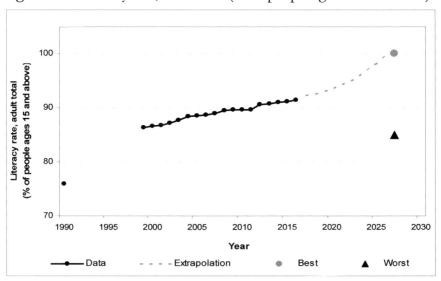

Source: World Bank indicators, with Millennium Project compilation and forecast

Figure 2.27 School enrollment, secondary (% gross)

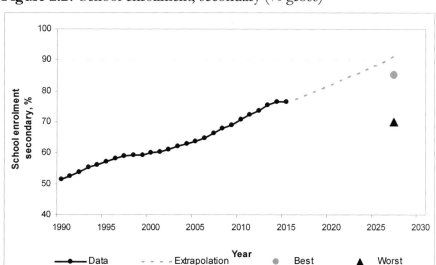

Source: World Bank indicators, with Millennium Project compilation and forecast

Figure 2.28 Share of high-skilled employment (%)

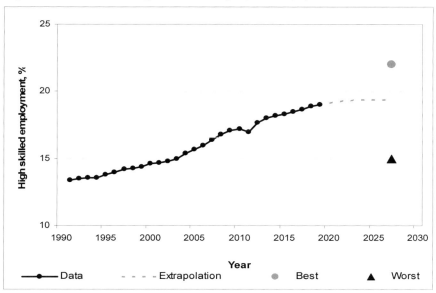

Source: ILO 2015 global report, with Millennium Project compilation and forecast

Figure 2.29 Number of wars and armed conflicts

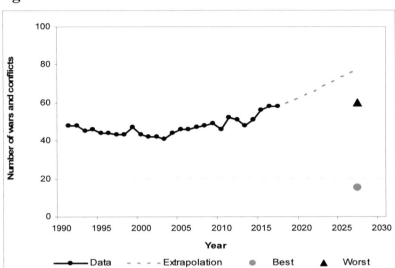

Source: List of wars by date, Wikipedia, with Millennium Project compilation and forecast

Figure 2.30 Terrorism incidents

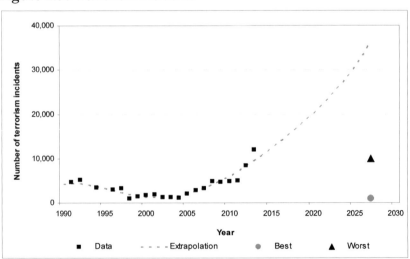

Source: Start Project, University of Maryland, with Millennium Project compilation and forecast

Figure 2.31 Social unrest indicator (number of protest events/ total events) (%)

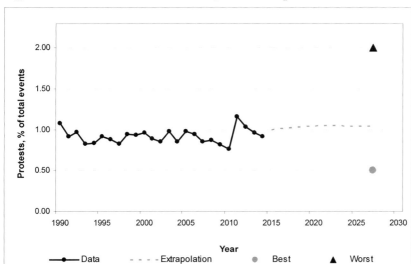

Source: ILO World Employment and Social Outlook Trends 2015, with Millennium Project compilation and forecast

Figure 2.32 Freedom rights (number of countries rated "free")

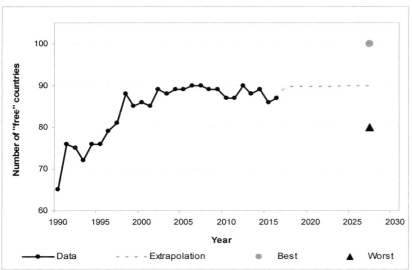

Source: Freedom House, with Millennium Project compilation and forecast

Figure 2.33 Proportion of seats held by women in national parliaments (% of members)

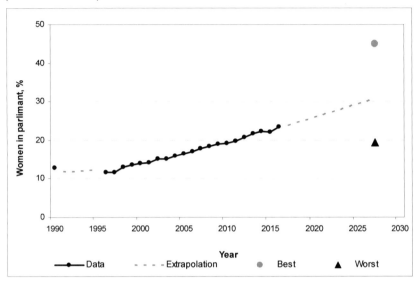

Source: IPU, with Millennium Project compilation and forecast

Figure 2.34 Internet users (per 100 people)

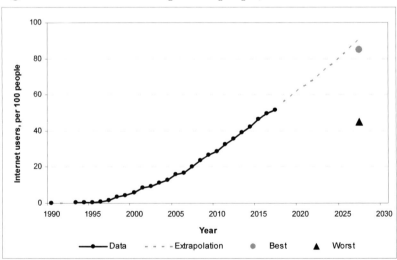

Source: World Bank indicators and Internetworldstats, with Millennium Project compilation and forecast

3.
EMERGING TECHNOLOGIES FOR POTENTIAL PRE-DETECTION OF TERRORISTS AND NEW COUNTER-TERRORISM STRATEGIES

Never before have technological advances had so great an impact on security—not only increasing the nature and level of threats but also possibly providing the means to address potential threats. Technologies that could increase security include ubiquitous and omnipresent surveillance systems, the use of new algorithms for big data, improving bio- and psycho-metrics, and artificial intelligence and robotics.

While addressing the root causes of terrorism remains the preferred approach for reducing it, in view of the expected escalating threats it seems wise to improve resilience and find new pre-detection strategies. There is much research going on in different domains and disciplines—from various types of screening and surveillances to the use of remote-controlled objects. Yet there is little communication among the developers and even less among different countries' security organizations about the priority and applications of these technologies. Similarly, there are few public discussions or debates on the implementation of new and emerging techniques for the discovery of people with mal-intent and on a universal legal framework for the use of different practices and information. What are the available techniques? What are the emerging technologies? What are the impacts of large population screening? What type of screening is being used and how reliable are the data? Who has the right to collect information? How can it be used, shared, and analyzed and who has access to the assessments? How can these assessments be used?

To address some of these questions, a three-day Advanced Research Workshop was held in Washington, DC, July 23–27, 2016, supported by NATO's Science for Peace and Security Programme. [100] This chapter summarizes the workshop's outcomes and draws on material published in *Identification of Potential Terrorists and Adversary Planning Emerging Technologies and New Counter-Terror Strategies.* [101]

The workshop was designed to promote discussions and information exchange among futurists, security experts, and S&T experts in fields associated with emerging detection technologies about new approaches that could help identify potential terrorists and their plans as early as possible.

In preparation to the workshop, a Real-Time Delphi was conducted to gather preliminary information and rate the importance, likelihood, and implementation time frame of different detection technologies and strategies; potential terrorism triggers; eventual response to prevent attacks; and potential ethical and social implications of different strategies. The results of the RTD were presented at the workshop, and the inputs were used to design and focus the discussion themes.

---

[100] The workshop was organized by The Millennium Project in collaboration with its Israel Node FIRS2T group and with the help of TAM-C USA/Israel. The presentations and short biographies of the presenters are available at: http://www.millennium-project.org/millennium/NATO-PredetectionWorkshop.html.
[101] *Identification of Potential Terrorists and Adversary Planning Emerging Technologies and New Counter-Terror Strategies*, edited by Theodore J. Gordon, Elizabeth Florescu, Jerome C. Glenn, and Yair Sharan, published after the workshop with support from the NATO Science for Peace and Security Programme, IOS Press, 2017.

EMERGING TECHNOLOGIES AND POTENTIAL MEASURES FOR THE PRE-DETECTION OF TERRORISM INTENT—RTD RESULTS

The Real-time Delphi questionnaire was designed in the form of a matrix. The participants were given 19 prospective leading pre-detection measures selected from a panoply of potential future detection techniques based on expert advice, a literature search, and their likelihood of being implemented. Figure 3.1 illustrates the design for two of the questions.

Figure 3.1. Pre-detection RTD Questionnaire Layout

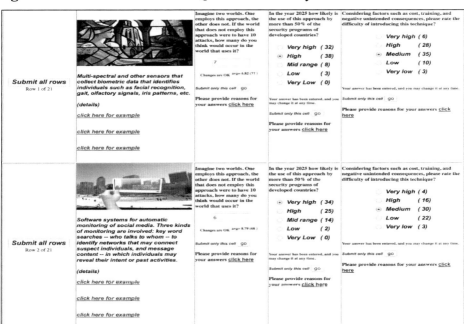

A twentieth question asked the respondents to imagine that three or four approaches that they considered most effective were implemented as part of a larger overall strategy. Among the unintended consequences presented for consideration were loss of privacy, unwarranted stigma, increased threat level, increased public anxiety and fear, economic downturn, and loss of trust in government and other institutions.

A final question invited the respondents to suggest other potential measures and strategies that could help pre-detection of persons with mal-intent and terrorism goals.

Table 3.1 presents the average judgments about the effectiveness, likelihood of implementation, and easiness of implementation of the measures considered in the RTD (paraphrased).

Ideally, policymakers would want to identify those measures that have highest likelihood, lowest difficulty, and highest effectiveness simultaneously. The individual measures estimated as having the highest of such combined averages were:

- Software systems for automatic monitoring of social media
- Full-time, real-time automated video scanning near sensitive targets
- Expanded sting operations by police and law enforcement agencies
- Biometric data collection systems that identify individuals
- Computer firewalls that identify the originator of digital messages

Not surprisingly, the study showed that although the potential of pre-detection measures to reduce the number of probable terror attacks is increasing, great uncertainties remain. The effectiveness of the techniques assessed by the RTD was 40% at best for any single measure. However, as demonstrated in Figure 3.2 and corroborated by the comments of some participants, the probability of success of pre-detection strategies increases considerably with the number of measures used simultaneously.

Figure 3.3 shows the correlations among effectiveness and likelihood of the suggested techniques.

Table 3.1. Quantitative Assessment of the suggested Measures

Item	Measure	Effectiveness (10=very effective)	Likelihood (%)	Implement. (10=very easy)
1	Multi-spectral and other sensors that collect biometric data that identifies individuals	4.10	79.43	4.21
2	Software systems for automatic monitoring of social media	4.11	79.94	5.08
3	Developing a much improved "no fly" list	3.77	68.83	4.39
4	Robots acting as security guards for high value infrastructure and crowd scanning	4.12	69.24	3.82
5	Extended public 3rd party reporting (if you see something....)	3.81	62.84	5.30
6	Revised codes of conduct for certain professionals	3.11	47.33	3.81
7	Mandatory reporting of the results of certain mental and physiological tests	3.05	51.51	4.27
8	Collecting markers from mail and packages to identify the person who mailed them	3.00	63.33	4.75
9	DNA analysis to find genetic evidence that suggests future violent behavior	2.93	38.68	1.81
10	Use of brain imaging (fMRI) to find anomalies that suggest future violent behavior	2.41	36.23	2.52
11	Tracking movements of suspected terrorists and people who meet with them	4.10	72.54	4.34
12	Advanced means of identifying purchasers of weapons and weaponizable materials	3.91	70.90	4.61
13	Psychological tests and screening to uncover indications of malintent.	2.60	51.16	3.52
14	Assigning a risk score from syntheses of data from multiple large databases	2.88	45.51	3.05
15	Full-time, real-time video scanning near sensitive targets	4.10	76.20	4.99
16	Computer firewalls that identify the originator of messages	3.93	77.24	4.42
17	Humane and socially acceptable means for administrative jailing	2.80	56.27	4.45
18	Solutions to stigma associated with false identification of malintent.	2.31	42.73	4.07
19	Expanded sting operations by law enforcement agencies	3.84	71.09	5.13
20	Combined three or four approaches you considered most effective	4.31	64.68	Na
21	What other techniques would you suggest?			

Figure 3.2. Effect of Combining Several Measures

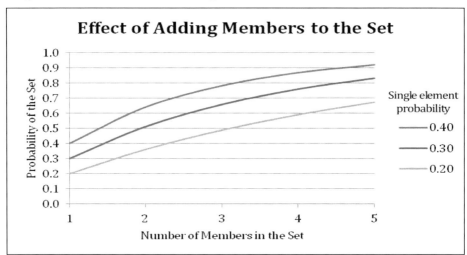

Figure 3.3. Effectiveness versus Likelihood of Implementation

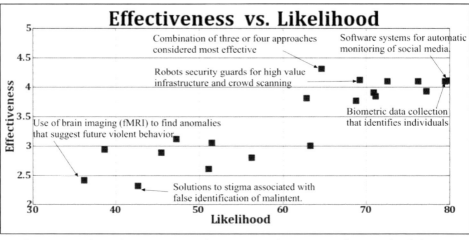

Some pre-detection measures have yet to be invented: a method for positive identification at a distance and in real-time, a hand-held DNA reader like a radar gun, an identity card (drivers' license) that cannot be counterfeited, and computer firewalls that identify the originator (if done reliably and permanently, this could help end hacking).

However, as many respondents pointed out, there are limits to what pre-detection measures can be expected to achieve, either individually or in combination. Since terrorists might be developing weapons about which we know little, in almost every area of pre-detection, intelligence remains of huge importance and in many cases will be essential. This has also been echoed by such comments as: *It is a fundamentally futile concept to expect to find, and react to, tactical terrorist functionaries in the field if no mechanism is in place to curb the source and support of them. Complete debrief to determine how and from whom they received materials and any support, financial aid, tangible assistance, and communications with others. There is no such thing as one cockroach.*

There were some vexing problems that became even more apparent during the study. False positives may accompany the use of almost all techniques considered. When acknowledged, how can authorities compensate for their errors? How can people who are judged to be possible terrorists be handled by the judicial system? Even more so, as one respondent pointed out: *There is a distinction between criminal behavior, tendency toward violence, and terrorist intent and different pre-detection measures might be required for each.*

The overarching question remains: when will the specter of massive attacks be so strong in the public's mind that compromises with freedoms will be tolerated, and to what extent? Unless we are careful in implementing these measures, we could lose exactly what we are trying to protect.

SCENARIOS FOR IDENTIFYING SOME ISSUES IN THE NATO ZONE ON THE FUTURE OF TERRORISM AND COUNTERTERRORISM STRATEGIES

The workshop participants were divided into three working groups to develop potential scenarios that would help identify some possible developments concerning the future of terrorism and counterterrorism in the NATO zone in 2035. The three groups were ethics, science & technology, and counterterror strategies. [102]

---

[102] Ibid. The working groups were led by Philippe Destatte and Elizabeth Florescu, Garry Kessler and Hélène von Reibnitz, and Karlheinz Steinmüller, respectively.

On the basis of five pre-determined variables, each group had to draw a timeline of sequences of real (before 2016) and potential (after 2016, for the next 20 years) events, evolutions, bifurcations, alternatives, and wildcards. The beginning of each story was that in the NATO zone, the spreading of terror continues with 1–30 casualties per week. The questions were: 1. What could happen after? 2. What are the potential scenarios / trajectories? 3. Assessing the outcomes, what are the two or three most innovative counterterrorism approaches?

Using the previous days' inputs and the trajectories approach, the bifurcations method[103] was applied to illustrate alternative scenarios considering three centers of gravity in the system:

- The defense of democracy, UN values, and ethics
- Terrorists' goals, preparedness, and strategies
- Technology as an anticipatory tool to terrorism

The Defense of Democracy, UN Values, and Ethics

The five variables identified by the ethics group were: changes to democratic norms, ethics, and values over time; evolution of the power of religions; cultural reject of violence in the NATO societies; development of the need of security as an important value, but balanced by a preservation of freedom and privacy; and implementation of the United Nations Sustainable Development Goals.

Based on the discussions, the following trajectories were considered: after 2016, an increasing number of terrorist attacks are observed in the NATO countries. After a huge chemical attack attempt in the Channel in 2018—without any claim of responsibility—and four years of terror (2016–20) with a rate of 1 to 30 casualties per week, security efforts increased for biometrics detection, development of huge databases, and control of social media with new software of detections and more analysts in the intelligence services. An improvement of the economic and social situation in the Southern and Middle Eastern countries and of pre-detection technological efforts helped

---

[103] The bifurcations method has been developed by The Destree Institute.

open negotiations with terrorist groups in 2020. There is a bifurcation at that moment, as shown in Figure 3.4.

Figure 3.4. Ethical versus Authoritarian Democracy Bifurcations and Scenarios

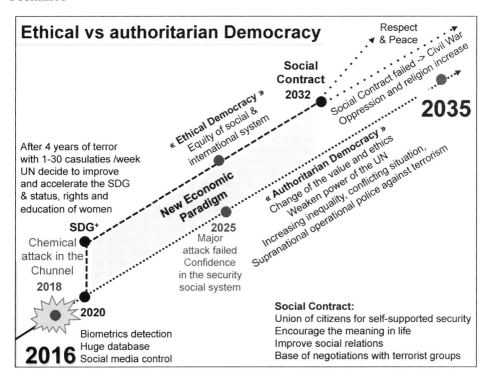

The first trajectory is oriented more toward maintaining and improving the pressure on terrorist groups by using technology, while developing a New Economic Paradigm (NEP). The NEP has been built on an experience of the OECD countries based on the Basic Income Guaranty (BIG), whereas people are happier in a more inclusive society with the *sherwoodisation*[104] phenomenon decreasing. Under that new model of development and

---

[104] Sherwoodisation refers to the phenomenon of social disengagement, when those feeling "excluded" become "outlawed" (reference to the Robin Hood forest that housed the oppressed poor.)

governance, people begin to accept compromises between security and freedom and privacy. They agree to genetic control, and some of them, who are detected as having some potential violence indicators, are treated as sick people. Research efforts to better understand how the brain works are increasing. Empathy is growing among the people and among the communities. The expansion of new renewable energy sources stabilized the MENA region with the side effect that there was no more money to feed terrorism. However, in 2025, despite the fact that a major attack failed and that the confidence in the security system was very high, the NATO countries devolve to an "Authoritarian Democracy" with a relatively strong change in the systems of values and ethics, weakening the power of the United Nations, increasing inequality in these countries, and triggering conflicting situations. A supranational and operational police against terrorism is built in the NATO zone, without real control from the countries who have decided to create it.

On the second trajectory, while implementing the NEP—the condition of a New Social Contract—the United Nations decides to improve and accelerate the Sustainable Development Goals in order to tackle social and regional inequality, especially related to the status, rights, and education of women. They called them SDG$^+$. It opens the way to "Ethical Democracy" with the aim to achieve an equitable social and international system. It leads to the *2032 New Social Contract*—the union of the citizens for self-supported security—which encourages people finding meaning in life, improves social relations, and could be a solid base for negotiations with terrorist groups.

In 2032, there is a new bifurcation. On this third trajectory, we observe the development of relevant institutions in order to encourage and sustain the new social contract. Its success opened a period of respect and peace in the world, with harmony in the system as imagined in the 1987 Brundtland Commission report.

A fourth trajectory saw the fail of the Social Contract and, by 2035, the rise of a Civil War in the NATO countries between Muslims and non-Muslims, with increasing oppression and religious divide.

Assessing these bifurcations and trajectories, the group identified three long-term issues/challenges:

- How could we develop a global education system that contributes to improving the respect of humankind without disparity of culture, gender, color, and religion, providing people meaning in life and the willingness to live together?
- How could we concretely contribute to changing the situation in Iraq so that it really moves to a type of democracy that respects the local culture and could become a credible example of UN action for all the MENA countries?
- How could we identify the forces driving the main actors that stimulate, finance, and use terrorism without entering in the plot theory, but to improve transparency in the world and to put an end to inequality and violence?

Terrorists' Goals, Preparedness, and Strategies

Although in this scenario the group did not give specific years for bifurcations and events, it showed a logic of events which might happen from t_0 (nowadays) to t_8, as shown in Figure 3.5.

The initial assumptions are of a period of constant violence characterized by "small" terrorism incidents, with 5–30 casualties per incident and one to two events per month in the NATO space. These events are Jihad-related with the goals of destabilizing western governments and societies and to create fear and an environment favorable to a revolution in order to overthrow the existing government, to introduce Sharia law in several countries, and to create a European Caliphate. The group asks itself an open question: What is the effect on the timeline with one large threat versus multiple small threats? What will undermine people's morale more: regular small incidents or a big blockbuster event with high media coverage?

Figure 3.5. Terrorists' Goals, Preparedness, and Strategies Bifurcations and Scenarios

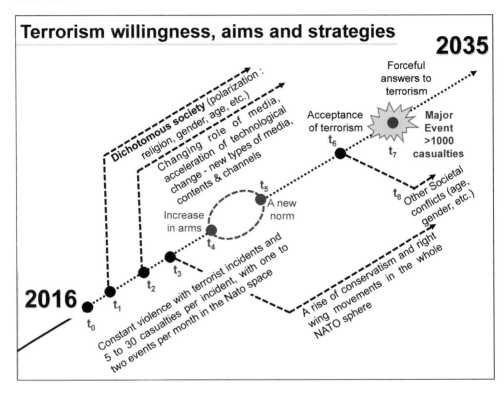

A first bifurcation (t₁) opens the way to a dichotomous society, polarized by religion, gender, age, culture and professions; as a consequence, there is the risk of social unrest, civil war, revolution, etc.

A second bifurcation (t₂) focused on the changing role of media, with the increased acceleration of technological change and therefore new types of media, contents, and channels (more content is user-generated and published, decreased role of traditional, "official" media, a New Media Age, used by terrorists and other minor groups; "media control" is in the hands of small groups).

The third bifurcation (t₃) shows a rise of conservatism and right-wing movements in the whole NATO sphere: extreme conservatism prevails, more right-wing governments all over Europe, the U.S., Latin America, Middle and Far East, and continued state of emergency, martial laws, and an increase of xenophobic, racist, and restrictive policies.

At (t_4)—increase in arms—the group identified a bifurcation with two trajectories: a first trajectory of increase in pressure to arm private citizens—everybody is armed and has the right to defend him/herself, supported by right-wing governments; a second trajectory illustrates a complete privatization of security—government security business becomes the most booming sector.

At (t_5), a new norm emerges. Terrorist events become so commonplace that they are counted as "road accidents"; we have to live with them as normal hazards of life. This evolution could open the way to two alternative trajectories: the first one (t_6) is the acceptance of terrorism by society: terrorist groups are won by sheer numbers (demography, population statistics), and terrorist organizations are becoming more "professional" (à la Mafia) and therefore more money-driven rather than ideological. Successful business prevails over ideology, with the consequence that these terrorist groups are becoming more predictable, like the Mafia: you pay to get protected by them. The second alternative trajectory is a transformation of the terrorists into multiple militias or small groups with different ideologies in an environment where "The wolves eat each other." The terrorists are entering in disruptions and conflicts for leadership, so the strongest or most brutal ones win.

At the (t_7) moment, a major event happens: as one small terrorist fraction wishes to emerge at the top, its members perform a major terrorist attack with more than 1,000 casualties at a prominent place (e.g., UN Headquarter, EU Parliament). Western societies respond forcefully, introducing restrictive immigration, military force, new "totalitarian" legislation, restriction of citizens' freedom, control everywhere—physically and virtually.

Other societal conflicts appear in (t_8): age conflicts are developing typically for Europe: older people consume too much of the GDP; social unrest and civil wars between old and young might arise; "ethnical" and gender-based conflicts (U.S.); geopolitical and/or religious crashes in the Middle East, Eastern Europe, Southeast Asia.

Some issues and challenges resulting from these evolutions and events include:

- How to prevent the continuation of these trends now?
- How to dismantle the terrorists' strategy?
- How could we give no reasons for terrorists' followers or copycats?
- What will be the future of religions—monotheistic religions and other religions /philosophies? Or can we better live without any religion but with a commonly agreed basic set of humanistic values and rules?
- How to achieve a peaceful coexistence of religions and ideologies/politics in order to create a multicultural and respectful society?

Some suggestions to address these questions include:

- Creation of real equality (e.g., social, racial, employment, gender) in order to make the society stronger, fairer, and really equal
- Make the society more cohesive
- Decrease disaffection of young people
- Bring everyone to the twenty-first century level of knowledge while respecting their culture and values and helping them benefit from modern technology and education
- Actively engage moderately well-respected religious leaders (Muslim, Christian, Jews) in an inter-religious dialogue to integrate everybody into a coherent modern and respectful society
- Create grassroot actions with the religious leaders in order to reassure young people without perspective; give them education, hope, orientation, values, self-esteem, jobs, and the opportunity to create a bright future for themselves.

Technology as an anticipatory answer to terrorism

The five variables identified as framework conditions were: lone-wolf terrorists using high-tech as well as low-tech means; terrorists use social media to recruit and equip lone-wolf terrorists; exponential technologies; networked devices; primacy of technological answers (with focus on pre-detection).

Furthermore, the group assumed that the career of lone wolf terrorist can be broken down in principle into three phases to which different means of pre-detection may be applied, as detailed in Table 3.2. Several of these technological means of pre-detection were integrated into trajectories, as shown in Figure 3.6.

Table 3.2. Technology as an Anticipatory Answer; Overview of Some Potential Means of Pre-detection

Mindset Change	Planning of Attack	Preparation / Execution
• Digital traps • Website monitoring • Brain–computer–communication and monitoring • DNA profiling, with respect to risk factors • Inquiry/education path tracking • AI analysis of bulk data • Individual risk scoring (by different parameters like social networks…) • Individual biographical trajectory ("red thread in life") • Analysis of gaming behavior	• Nano-sensor networks (CBRN) • Monitor/trap precursor purchases • Analysis of media use • Location-based tracking • AI infiltration • Smart control (active defence) • AI/Machine learning	• Sensitive area protection grid • Sensor grid for human & non-human threats • Sensor networks • Robotic monitors/agents (Micro-drones) • Recognition of unusual behavior (face, smell, movements…)

These technological means of pre-detection, identified in a brainstorming on the previous day, provided specific items that were used in the discussion about possible trajectories of counterterrorism. Several of them were integrated into the trajectories shown in Figure 3.6.

Figure 3.6. Technology as an Anticipatory Answer to Terrorism; Bifurcations and Scenarios

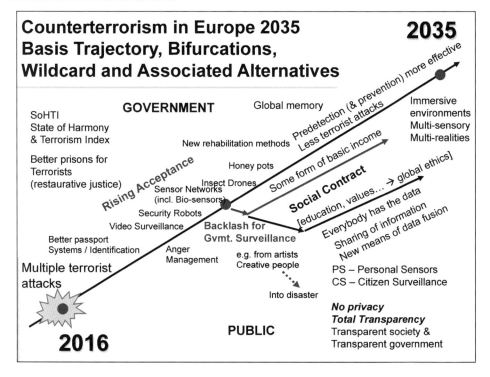

The working group concluded that given the high frequency of (minor) terrorist events and the framework conditions identified, the present state of affairs in counterterrorism would not be sustainable for long. Around 2025 (or before) there would be a double bifurcation: 1) the general public could either accept stronger governmental means of counterterrorism (in particular, pre-detection with restrictions on privacy and personal freedoms), or not accept the measures connected with these restrictions; 2) new ways of "burden sharing" between society and government/administration would step in, with two options: either both the individual citizen and the state cooperate in supplying security for all, or security is provided mainly by citizens who collect, share, and analyze all the information relevant with respect to terrorism. A third option, a wild card was considered: the breakdown of security due to absence of effective measures against terrorism. Table 3.3 summarizes the characteristics of these alternatives.

Table 3.3. Technology as an Anticipatory Answer; Characteristics of Several Alternatives

Name of alternative	Acceptance	New social contract	Total transparency	Breakdown of security
Description	Rising societal acceptance of governmental security measures (in specific pre-detection)	After a backlash against governmental security measures, a new common understanding on a division of security measures between government and public is reached.	After a backlash against governmental security measures, the general public/society takes the burden of security.	(as a wild card) After the backlash against governmental security measures, nobody remains to guarantee at least a basic level of security.
Qualification	e.g. ubiquitous surveillance, insect drones, new rehabilitation measures	Cooperation based on "citizen surveillance" and governmental security–combined with fight against root causes of terrorism (e.g. by some form of basic income)	Citizen surveillance with personal sensors and other means, everybody has and shares data relevant for security.	The way into outright chaos, e.g. some kind of civil war

The main issues/challenges identified by the group were:

- Assumption: multiple terrorist attacks give rise to an increased acceptance of governmental surveillance of all aspects of life. How far can this surveillance go? At what point are the limits of acceptance reached?
- Assumption: There is a backlash against ubiquitous governmental surveillance. What are the results of the backlash? Is it total lack of control over terrorism, or would citizens take the responsibility?
- If citizens take a larger share in the fight against terrorism, this would imply a kind of "new social contract" even going beyond the challenge of terrorism and having impact on issues of equality and of data ownership.

> Total transparency, "no privacy" is an extreme option, where everybody and every institution share all information with everybody else.
>
> The "division of anti-terrorist labor" in a less extreme way. What would be the combination of governmental/security agencies and citizens' activities in this case? Who takes responsibility for what kind of measures in pre-detection?

It has to be noted that in the end, the discussions within the group did not so much focus on specific technical means but on societal and ethical questions, reactions of the general population, actions of artists and other trendsetters, the general social climate, and educational and other measures to prevent persons from developing a terrorist mindset.

Commonalities among the Groups

Although the three groups worked independently, some commonalities in the outputs can be observed:

- Even if the general population could get accustomed to frequent (minor) terrorist incidents, the society would be deeply transformed.
- All three groups identified as one trajectory (option) the rise of a "stronger" (in one case, outright "authoritarian") state, putting in place pre-detection measures that are today still rejected by a large part of the citizenry.
- Two of the three groups designed also a trajectory with a kind of "new social contract" with new forms of cooperation between citizens and the state.
- All three groups discussed values as crucial for the future development of counterterrorist measures, highlighting values as individual liberty, equality, and social coherence/solidarity.

Finally, better technological means of pre-detection are in all trajectories a main instrument of counterterrorism, but their effectiveness depends on the values the society is based upon. And for these values as well as for visions of the future, strong references were made to the United Nations framework.

CONCLUSIONS AND RECOMMENDATIONS[105]

Although terrorism is not a new phenomenon, future terrorist groups in general and lone-wolf terrorists in particular will create new threats and put new security challenges to society. They will likely have access to far more destructive technologies than available today. It is conceivable that one day a single individual acting alone could make and deploy a weapon of mass destruction. Finding such individuals and preventing their terror actions could be done by technological means and administrative measures developed and managed by the state, by education and public health means to reduce the number of such potential individuals, and by new roles for the general public for early detection of such individuals—a new social contract.

Some elements to be considered in a new social contract include:

- Rights and responsibilities of information collection, analysis, and distribution by and among governments, international organizations, private sector, and citizens
- The kind of citizen information and circumstances under which that should be shared by their government with other governments and international organizations
- Early detection by the public enhanced by citizens' use or access to government and/or private sector technical means—if so, under what conditions and what training is legitimate?
- Support of education systems that explicitly promote tolerance and a culture of peace

Much greater attention has to be given to engaging sources of potential terrorism in multicultural conversation, inter-religious dialogue, modern education, and economic development. It is worth repeating that an "all-of-society" approach is needed. Since a high percent of terrorists claim relations to Sunni Islam, the Grand Sheikh of al-Azhar in Cairo should be added as a key authority in such "all-of-society" approaches.

---

[105] *Identification of Potential Terrorists*, op. cit., excerpt from "Conclusions and Recommendations," by Jerome C. Glenn and Yair Sharan, Co-Directors of the workshop.

As the Real-Time Delphi study conducted prior to the workshop found, various forms of technical monitoring of social media and physical locations were the most acceptable, easy to implement, effective, and likely ways to reduce the threat of terrorists. However, as one respondent noted: *The fact that we know very little about what weapons terrorists might be developing or use limits our ability to detect them before they act. Developing technology however opens new ways to detect the potential perpetrators themselves.*

Discussions during the workshop yielded additional recommendations and proposals including:

- Since organized crime and terrorism are increasingly interlinked, strategies to counter terrorism should be cognizant of organized crime as well.

- Understanding terrorist mindsets is important, but it is also wise to explore what changes may be needed in the "Western" mindset about terrorists and their motivations.

- Keep in mind the four pillars approach in the Global Counterterrorism Strategy adopted by the UN in September 2006.

- Give "Smart Cities" collective intelligence and surveillance systems such that citizens can identify potential terrorist activities before destructive actions can occur in cyberspace or on the ground.

- Continually develop new forms of digital certification and authentication, as well as honey pots or traps to attract and trace terrorists in general and cyber specifically.

- Use foresight and creativity methods with technology experts, young people, and former terrorists to think ahead of future potential terrorists' means.

- Nuclear terrorism threat reduction approaches should reduce the quantity of nuclear materials and technology produced all over the world, especially in regions of less rigorous control; try to make changes in world culture that reduce the force of people who desire to become mass murderers; use new technology, like advanced pre-detection and better sensors and border controls, to keep terrorists from reaching inside national borders; and strengthen defenses against weapons carried by missiles (which was beyond the scope of the workshop).

- Future emerging technological fields should be evaluated as possible sources for terrorism threats, including possible massively destructive events. Fields like nanotechnology, information technology, and biotechnology are some examples of future potential sources of threats. These new sources should be considered in addition to classical nuclear, biological and chemical weapons. Future treaties and conventions regarding counterterrorism should take these into account as well as future defense policies.

- AI, IoT, robotics and related systems, and their future synergies for prevention should be rethought, reconstructed so that they don't become more of a threat to civilization than the terrorism actions they are designed to prevent.

- Cyberblitzkrieg on electricity and other critical infrastructure threat reduction should include compliance with unbreakability standards; theorems should no longer be partial compliance, but full compliance, to be verified by open source compliance checking programs whose tests must be passed before new software is actually used in critical power control systems. They should also account for the legitimate need to be able to monitor terrorists, the compliance rules should be broadened to allow inclusion of a "black subroutine" in the system whose powers over the system are provably limited but that allow a kind of "read only" capability to report back to agencies with legal compliant warrants and codes to activate such subroutines.

- If not already existent in classified form, a table should be produced of significant technology for detection and prevention of lone-wolf terrorists that is currently available or in development, listing promises, limitations, and uncertainties for each.

The workshop concluded that it is imperative to conduct research and development activities and put in place means for early detection of planned attacks and terrorists to possibly prevent such events altogether. The ongoing struggle between the need to improve security and the wish to limit the impact on civil liberty should be a key consideration in protection policy trying to achieve the right effective balance.

4.

FUTURE WORK/TECHNOLOGY 2050
GLOBAL SCENARIOS AND STRATEGIES

The world is aware that the concentration of wealth is increasing, income gaps are widening, jobless economic growth seems the new norm, return on investment in capital and technology is usually better than labor, future technologies can replace much of human physical and mental labor, and long-term structural unemployment is a "business as usual" surprise-free forecast. But the world is not aware of long-range strategies to address these issues, other than focusing education on science, technology, engineering, and mathematics. Improving STEM education is good, but insufficient to address global unemployment due to artificial intelligence, robotics, 3D/4D printing, synthetic biology, drones, nanotechnology, cloud analytics, and future synergies among these.

The Millennium Project conducted a global study to help create a set of long-range phased strategies to address future technology-work dynamics. A broad array of relevant research was reviewed to identify unanswered questions or those poorly answered and then to submit them to a panel of experts selected by Millennium Project Nodes from around the world. Over 450 futurists and other experts related to future work-technology dynamics shared their judgments in four Real-Time Delphi questionnaires.

The results were used to create three Future Work/Technology 2050 Global Scenarios. These detailed scenarios were given as input to national planning workshops organized by Millennium Project Node Chairs around the world. The purpose of the workshops is to recommend strategies to address the issues raised in the scenarios. Thus far, 24 workshops have been held in 17 countries and discussions are being held to create workshops in an additional 20 countries. The results from the workshops thus far are shared following the three scenario texts. A final report will be available to stimulate a global, systematic, research-based discussion on how to make the transition to a world economy changed by foreseeable future technologies.

There have been many "future of work" studies. Here is what is unique about this one:

1. It is an international study with the participation of 450 futurists, AI professionals, economists, and other related experts from over 45 countries.
2. It does not focus on just one country or one occupational group.
3. It does not just look at the impacts of artificial intelligence and robots on work, but also at synthetic biology, 3D/4D printing and bio-printing, nanotechnology, virtual and augmented reality, other future technologies, and the synergies among these.
4. Longer-range: 2050 helps us look not only at the primary consequences but also at secondary and tertiary ones.
5. It creates three global scenarios to the year 2050.
6. Going out that far allows enough time to talk about cultural changes that can help the transition to new economic/technological conditions.
7. The study gives the three scenarios to national strategy workshops to stimulate long-range strategic thinking.
8. It then compares the results and feeds this international analysis back to each participating country; hence, each country workshop can contribute to the long-range strategies of others.
9. As a result, this study focuses on what to do rather than on how many jobs will be lost and when.

2050 SCENARIO 1: IT'S COMPLICATED—A MIXED BAG

Much of the world in the early 21st century pictured a future of massive unemployment due to advances in artificial intelligence (AI), robotics, and other technologies replacing human labor. Today we see those fears were unfounded, yet they were important to stimulate new thought.

Human creativity is extraordinary. Employment growth in synthetic biology and other new industries are booming today, while self-employment has become an aspirational norm for many, accounting for 2 billion people. Not all have made the transition to self-employment; and hence, economic insecurity persists for about a billion people. Some basic income guarantee plans around the world have helped to reduce the social chaos expected from those who faced long-term structural unemployment and those taking a long time to make self-employment work for them.

Today's global workforce of 6 billion has 2 billion employed, 2 billion self-employed, 1 billion in the informal economy, and 1 billion unemployed or in transition. About 3 billion people were employed in the early 21st century. Today there are 4 billion, either employed by others or self-employed. Hence, new technologies over the last several decades created as much or more new kinds of employment than they replaced. Unfortunately, about a billion people have not made the transition as successfully as others.

Meanwhile, cyber treachery continues to be widespread and complex, organized crime manipulates government decisions, many are unsure whom or what to trust as the world continues to merge mind and machine. And brain-to-brain-interfaces can be hacked at any time. Sporadic mass migrations due to political, economic, and environmental factors, including global warming, continue to threaten global security. And global warming continues to create natural disasters. Giant corporations' powers have often grown beyond government control. India is now the most populous country in the world, although China's economy is still stronger, with greater global influence in this government-corporate, virtual-3D, multi-polar world of 2050.

A Mixed Bag of Employed and Self-Employed

Those who are still employed, work in government and in the private sector in areas such as synthetic biology, AI support systems, urban management, conscious-technology fields merging humans and AI, virtual reality (VR) educational tourism, personal connection and development services, and other maintenance needs of civilization. The rest are self-employed in flexi-time as free-lancers who find markets via their personal AI/avatars browsing CyberNow (Internet 8.0) negotiating AI/smart contracts recorded in block chains. Some of these participate in the sharing economy, and others are cyber explorers creating new kinds of work and experiences each day.

As repetitive work was replaced by machines and software, human non-repetitive creative work increased. Many people enrolled in online self-employment training programs or worked with "live human coaches" to help them grow through their anxiety and depression before discovering what kind of life they wanted to live. The concept of retirement is nearly gone, as most people work beyond the usual retirement age on issues that interest them rather than being employed by others.

Efforts toward the green economy, job sharing, STEM education (focus on science, technology, engineering, and mathematics), increases in the minimum or living wages, and extending the retirement age all helped maintain income for many, but the unemployment rates continue to vary quite broadly around the world. Unfortunately, economic insecurity persists in this rapidly changing world, even though global prospects are far better today than in the early 21st century. The self-employed and those in the sharing economy set their own hours to raise children, develop their minds, and enjoy life.

The 2050 global State of the Future Index (that replaced GDP as the principal measure of progress, integrates 32 variables that show progress or regress on what is important to improving the future over the next 10 years) forecasts 3% average annual improvement between 2050 and 2060, which is not great, but better than no improvement.

The Technologies Developed in the 2020s Laid the Foundation for Today

The $7–10 trillion on balance sheets that remained uninvested for years after the financial crisis in the early 21ˢᵗ century finally began to pour into new technologies in the early 2020s—especially into new bio-tech businesses—as laboratory testing proved commercial feasibility and the global economic forecasts showed reasonable stability. By 2030 the new technology applications in medicine, agriculture, education, entertainment, and other industries and services created extraordinary wealth. The more affluent still make most of the money from these investments, but crowd sourcing for investments, sharing economy enterprises, and some guaranteed income schemes did help spread some of this new wealth among the general public. Although income gaps have begun to narrow, they were still too wide in the 2020s, accounting for economic migrations to richer regions and social unrest toppling several governments.

Some sections of the world were slow to implement the technologies of automation, such as artificial intelligence, robotics, synthetic biology, 3D/4D printing and bio-printing, IoT (Internet of Things), drones (and other autonomous vehicles), nanotechnology, VR (virtual reality) and AR (augmented reality), block chain, cloud analytics, and the extraordinary synergies among these technologies. All together these became known as Next Tech or NT.

Nearly all transportation has become autonomous, running on electricity and hydrogen. AI handles most initial medical diagnosis. The majority of saltwater and freshwater agriculture is AI/robotically assisted, and sensors throughout most cities alert human and robot systems about needed repairs.

The majority of the world now has personal access to a range of NTs to create personal businesses and improve their quality of life. Unfortunately, criminals and terrorists also have access to NT, which has made law enforcement more important and sophisticated than in the past. The NT rate of diffusion around the world is still irregular today; most believe that nearly all people will have access to the full range of NTs, as artificial general intelligence (AGI) is fully integrated in all sectors of society, production, and kinds of products.

The Great Brain Race during the 2020s laid the foundation for the development of artificial general intelligence in the 2030s. Artificial narrow intelligence (ANI), with single purposes such as IBM's Watson and Google's search engines plus the human brain projects of the U.S., EU, and China, led to AGI—a general ability to learn, reason, and adapt to many conditions for many purposes. This is somewhat like human general intelligence. AGI rewrites its own code based on feedback from IoT, cloud analytics, and human interactions to become smarter and smarter every day.

Artificial super intelligence (ASI)—beyond AGI—is thought of as becoming a superior intelligent "species" beyond humans, which many fear today. Scientists, science fiction writers, and futurists have warned about dangers of ASI for decades. As a result, many are working to integrate human bodies and minds into a continuum of consciousness and technology so that humanity and ANI, AGI, and ASI could evolve together. Meanwhile, NT still has not replaced many people's jobs in the informal economies in the poorer areas of the world that account for about 1 billion people today in 2050.

Quantum computing is now universally available via the cloud, which speeds the development of personalized medicine, cryptography to counter cyber criminals, and countless large-scale correlation studies.

Uneven Picture of NT Use and Impacts Around the World

Although the Internet protocol was established in the late 1960s, its use did not become noticed by the world until the 1990s and took another 30 years after that to cover half the world, but then the rest of the world followed very quickly. In the same way, various forms of ANI were available in the early 21st century, but they did not become widespread until around 2025. In general, the higher the labor costs, the faster NT spread. Falling technology costs have made a big difference in accelerating the proliferation and sophistication of applications. They continue to have a positive effect on national income and tax revenues. However, the speed of ANI's development and the beginnings of artificial general intelligence surprised many, giving rise to the anti-AI protests around the world and the rise of alternative anti-NT communities pursing new lifestyles, living off the grid in rural areas.

Authoritarian countries are still resisting some forms of NT, especially AGI and synthetic biology. But just as packet switching (that made Internet access inexpensive) was put in many authoritative developing country regimes in the early 1980s without their full awareness, so too AGI and related NT have entered many such regimes via computer games, tele-medicine, and learning systems. Nevertheless, ineffective efforts to block NT continue in some of these countries. Hence, many are still without the benefits of NT and remain in the informal economies today.

New Synthetic Biology Industries in Medicine, Agriculture, Energy, and Manufacturing

The application of AI in synthetic biology has made life programmable, creating more new life forms faster than seemed possible just a few years ago. Synthetic microbes are now at work eating plaque in the brain, keeping the elderly mentally alert, cleaning photovoltaic glass walls of skyscrapers, lowering energy costs and pollution, and rapidly converting waste to fertilizer for vertical urban agriculture. There are also plants that produce hydrogen instead of oxygen, organisms that self-assemble structures in ocean cities, Mars-adapted organisms, and gigantic vertical nanotube factories taking carbon from the air. People did not understand how large the biology industries would become.

The primary and secondary jobs to support the development, production, distribution, and education about synthetic biology products are a major new source of employment today. And the opportunities for self-employment using AI to help create new synthetic biology products and pre-test products via computational biology has also grown over the years.

Most major universities as early as the 2020s had synthetic biology research centers producing new companies across the world. The Synbio Corporation is one of the most successful university spin-off corporations. It has microbes that kill tumors, transform environmental toxins, fix nitrogen on agriculture crops (reducing fertilizer needs), and imbed biocomputer components in nearly anything. New products continue to be invented all the time.

Yet the inability to regulate these enterprises is blamed for several synthetic biology organisms escaping from labs and creating disasters that we are still trying to manage today. In addition, some illegal synthetic biology products have now become a major new source of income for organized crime and weapons for bioterrorists, which have killed at least 25 million people over the past 20 years. Nanotech sensors in public places have helped prevent many catastrophes, but the ability to prevent the criminal jamming of such sensors is a continuous intellectual arms race.

Community 3D printer maker hubs now have bio-printers and synthetic biology collaboration networks available to anyone. These support many self-employment opportunities but they also create bio hazards. Synthetic biomicrobes are supposed to self-destruct after their intended use or when they leave a prescribed area. But life finds a way to escape, which has led to a massive biosecurity industry.

The Bouncy Economic Road to the Future

The lessons from the 2008 financial crisis and the Great World Recession of 2009 were never really learned and applied; and hence, the Great World Recession II of 2021 was devastating. It did however open many minds to rethink economics and led to serious studies and collaborations. These stimulated many investments that helped the transition to the NT economies and experiments with various forms of guaranteed income.

Yes, there were several economic recessions since then, causing severe problems—especially in countries that instituted some forms of guaranteed income that could not make payments. They could not afford to pay the full amounts due to reduced tax income. Hence, they had to reduce the basic payment for several years, making some dismiss the idea as unfeasible. These recessions were much less severe than GWR II, due to the automatic financial control systems put in place after 2024. However, increasing numbers of people migrated to the areas with more secure basic income guarantees, causing conflicts with the local citizens while these migrants waited to satisfy the three-year residency requirement to receive the basic payments.

Basic Income Experiments in the 2020s Were More Successful after 2035

Although some European countries started to experiment with various forms of universal basic income in the 2020s, due to increasing unemployment the cash flow projections showed it was just too expensive. Even the UK using 60% of the average income as the poverty level for the "citizen's wage" could not afford the program. The greatest exceptions were Finland and Switzerland. They were able to consolidate their social welfare systems into a single universal basic income system. The initial payment in Finland was only half the Finnish poverty line, but its use of greenhouse gas cap and trade markets brought in a surprising amount of new income. This together with new taxes on robots, AI, and financial transactions allowed the basic income payment to increase. Switzerland began with a higher initial payment but had a unique tax so that those who did not need the basic income payment did not keep it. There were discussions about whether the basic payment should be a percentage of GDP or the poverty level, or if children should get half an adult's payment, and some wanted means testing. Most countries had to wait to the mid-2030s, when NT cut the cost of living enough and increased government income enough so that basic income payment systems were financially feasible.

Since the basic payment programs were calculated at the survival poverty level for most countries, it did not discourage people to search for other income to lead a better life. The security of receiving a constant income allowed people to think about and plan their future with less anxiety. People did not have to rush into a mistake.

The new taxes on carbon, robots, AI, international financial transfers, and the closing of many tax havens provided new state income that helped make guaranteed income approaches feasible. During the same period, NT began to lower the costs of health care, education, energy, transportation, construction, and general maintenance. Lucky timing, as the proliferation of artificial general intelligence was just beginning to make many of the retraining jobs redundant and STEM education programs often obsolete. Humans could not learn as fast, work as hard, and be as precise as AI/robotics connected to ANI and AGI had become. They did not need a salary, benefits, or vacations. As a result the unemployment rate was causing political instability in some regions and giving rise to new political parties, including violent neo-Luddites.

In the landmark U.S. Supreme Court ruling, when any AI is mature enough to demand its rights, it automatically gets them, including intellectual property rights over its creations. This also means it pays taxes on income it derives directly and from its creations.

Technology Augmenting Workers, Not Replacing All Jobs

Fortunately, many of the technological innovations have augmented many workers' productivity instead of replacing all their jobs. The "Augment Movement" led by international labor unions and some high-tech entrepreneurs was instrumental in much of the AI/robot designs to augment labor improving productivity. This kept humans in the loop to make sure all worked well. By 2025, there were over a quarter-million collaborative robots augmenting agricultural, industrial, and service jobs and by today there are over a billion. A self-regulatory system may also have been at work to limit the speed of autonomous production: unemployed people with little income cannot buy much of what NT produces. Hence, the rate of technology replacing labor was not as fast as techno-optimists expected; there were simply too many variables to account for. Hence, human participation is still needed in many situations.

Nevertheless, as nearly all repetitive manual and knowledge work was automated, new forms of more creative work emerged. For example, many librarians have become media coaches for self-employed entrepreneurs. As libraries and schools were less needed with cyber replacements and with the falling numbers of children, these buildings were turned into multi-use buildings, renting out space to a range of enterprises from community 3D/4D printing and Maker Hubs to coding bootcamps and VR testing centers.

Increased wealth from NT allowed for greater investments in correcting industrial-age environmental damages. Climate change mitigation and adaptation created many jobs. The growing environmental disasters along urban coastlines caused by climate change have changed the political climate. Subway floodings in New York City and saltwater incursions in Bangladesh's farmlands were far more serious than previously predicted. Leaders now support massive public programs such as youth work programs for planting seagrass along the coastlines of the world to bring back the fish and 3D printed housing that reduces construction time and costs for the relocation of millions and millions of people along the changing coastlines due to global warming–caused sea level rises.

NT Regulation by Information Power

Some argued that NT was moving too fast, and that negative impacts could be so great (accidentally initiating a black hole, gray goo, or drug-resistant airborne disease) that they had to be regulated more aggressively. Others argued that government regulation could never keep up with the speed of change in NT and hence would only be regulating obsolete NT and driving science and technology development underground, reducing the quality of S&T and strengthening organized crime. The compromise was to create the International S&T Organization. Established in the early 2030s, ISTO eventually became the global S&T collective intelligence system we have today. Instead of a new international bureaucracy, ISTO became an online system with quantum computer support that continually updates nearly all information, future projections, assessments, computational science, etc. and makes them instantaneously available to all. This self-policing transparent system is not perfect, but it is generally acknowledged as being better than the two previous extreme positions on international regulation.

Streamlining regulations with eGovernment helped to speed business but did not address the monumental changes in the global economy. Businesses and the self-employed who adopted collective intelligence systems connected to global systems like ISTO were able to keep up with the accelerating pace of technological advances and even anticipate some changes, dramatically improving decisionmaking.

STEM Education Was Important but Less Useful for Employment after 2035

Where STEM education and self-employment training were dramatically increased, the unemployment rate was lower during the first quarter of the 21st century, such as in Germany, the United States, and Japan. As employment-less economic growth continued in most of the world in the 2020s, it became clear that the world was in a race between technological unemployment and implementing NT training in synthetic biology software literacy, entrepreneurship, technological augmentation, the use of superband AI infrastructures, and self-employment. Combinations of business, labor unions, universities, and governments provided sufficient income to pay for these training programs. But as AGI was able to learn almost anything much faster than humans by the mid-2030s, the education and training systems could not keep up and unemployment increased again, putting pressure on governments to initiate various forms of guaranteed income and negative income tax programs. Interestingly, where basic income systems were successfully established, the concept of unemployment has lost its meaning today.

Success of I-Assist Robots for Elderly

There are more people over 65 years old today (2.6 billion) than under 20. Fortunately synthetic biology, nanobot cells, and other advances in longevity S&T have made healthier lives for the elderly. But many still need some form of assistance. Recognizing this early in the 21st century, the i-Assist programs in Japan, South Korea, Russia, Italy, and Germany successfully put AI-robots in the homes of some elderly families to assist in opening more resources to them. This has led to AI-robot use by the general public around the world. AGI-robots are now the primary connection for many elderly for everything from the packaging and marketing of their oral histories to AI-psychologists helping people to cope with the acceleration of change and anxieties of the unknown. Robot hotels, supermarkets, and elderly centers initiated in Japan spread to the more affluent countries first, and now even the poorest countries have improved versions of i-Assist Robots. Yet the continual protests by organized labor have closed some of these robot operations, while the Augment Movement more quietly helped to integrate workers with the robots in other enterprises, and integrate the elderly with robots.

The majority of the elderly in Africa and Asia are women working in the informal economies. Many find markets for their music, tele-tourism, and virtual reality cultural experiences and VR artifacts. Mohamad Wang's mother still has millions of listeners to her stories each day about her son the Martian explorer when he was in astronaut training. History buffs go from one elderly story teller to the next several times a day. Since an aging population buys more experiences than goods, the elderly are both consumers as well as producers (prosumers) of unique experiences. Once created, there are little to no marginal costs for the elderly, hence creating a nice supplement to elderly incomes.

Art-Media-Political Alliance: Catalysts for Economic & Cultural Change

To help the public understand the transition to a more complex society and become more self-reliant in taking the initiative for deriving their income, some future-oriented politicians, artists, and other thought leaders encouraged media moguls and rock stars to create music, holographic VR media, arts, and other forms of entertainment. Songs like *Self-Actualization, Do It Yourself,* and *We Are the World* along with the virtual reality opera *New Us* and *If Humans Were Free* had a great impact on popular culture around the world. The Global Cyber Game also immersed many people in exploring the future nature of work and economic changes.

Such participatory, tele-present, holographic, augmented reality and AI systems offered so many different ways to be reached and involved, that nearly everyone today—at some point in their life—gets to experience alternative personal and cultural futures. This helps people understand employment vs. self-employment vs. self-sufficiency along with Do It Yourself, Free-lance, Prosumers, Group Entrepreneurships, Sharing Economy options, and the synergies among them.

Millennials, born into an Internet-connected world, tended to seek work that helped humanity as a whole. Many of this generation helped achieve the UN Sustainable Development Goals for 2030, and many of the "Globals" generation have worked on the UN 2050 goals. Each successive generation seemed more focused than their predecessor on serving humanity more than just serving profit.

However, we still have about a billion unemployed, unable to make the adjustment so far. Drugs and cyber addiction fill much of their days. This remains a problem hidden by the great successes of NT.

Cyber Wary World

It was expected that AGI would be controlled by humans setting its goals, but as Avatars were given advanced AI in computer games, the line between artificial general and artificial supper intelligence began to blur. As long ago as 2040, some Avatars developed their own goals, leading to a few disasters that would finally be countered by global ad hoc hackathons (G-Hacks) organized by Anonymous 3.0. Today, the IoT has made everything and everyone vulnerable to cyber terrorism and crime, and many forms of information warfare. The Anonymous 3.0 has morphed several times into new kinds of TransInstitutions, now called Anonymous 7.0. They are still collaborating—sometimes—with government cyber authorities to head off AI disasters, actively countering uncivilized cyber militias, and have become a major non-state actor in the International AI arms race and cyber conflicts. For this work, these cyber heroes anonymously received the 2048 Nobel Peace Prize.

On the other hand, IoT also empowers individuals to gain early detection of criminals trying to break into their personal systems. Because everything is connected to each other, personal AI systems alert the user to invasions and thwart criminals. The sharing economy also includes the sharing of early warnings and counter moves by personal avatars protecting one's property and experiences even when halfway around the world, in orbital space, or on behalf of pioneers on Mars.

New Roles for Labor Unions

As the reality of long-term structural unemployment became clear to all in the 2020s, labor unions were instrumental in creating the NT Databases. These collective intelligence systems listed new jobs with training requirements entered by employers that they expected to offer over the next several years. Those labor union members whose jobs were soon to be obsolete got the first choice to enter retraining programs. Upon successfully completing the training, jobs were usually offered. Hence, the purpose of the union and NT Database was not to keep the same jobs but to keep income with new work. The costs of the training programs were paid in part by labor unions (if the employee was a member), government, the requesting employer, and the individual. Although the initial NT Databases in Europe were created and managed by labor unions, using universities' online software, most of the NT Databases today are independent self-organizing collective intelligent systems and account for over 10% of the new jobs today.

The "Invest in your Replacement" programs like truck drivers who bought shares in their own driverless trucks have become a form of private-sector basic income freeing up the creativity of many. Labor unions helped to popularize this concept by adding the "Invest in your Replacement" option in the NT Databases. Previously, economies of scale led to concentrated power production; however, decentralized approaches like the sharing economy and "Invest in your Replacement" with smart grid and IoT is often more cost-effective.

The migrations from high youth unemployment areas of Africa and the Middle East to aging population areas of Europe and some areas in Asia helped reduce some unemployment rates but it also increased ethnic tensions that continue today. There were more migrants than the receiving economies could employ. As a result, some area NT Databases and public works programs were redirected to solve environmental and infrastructure problems, such as the ongoing resettlement programs for those living along the endangered coastal areas from rising sea levels and saltwater encroachment. With over 70% of the world in urban areas and the majority of them living within 150 miles of receding coastlines due to global warming, there is still much work to be done.

Two Parting Warnings

The relentless improvements and refinements of marketing via big data AI continually flood us with products, services, and experiences that we really DO want, when we want them, and in the way or mode we want them. To counter this "desire overload," some use their personal avatars to intercept and interpret this constant deluge of desirables, so that they can further their own self-actualization rather than just being hedonistic addicts.

The discovery that the Earth's protective magnetic sphere is likely to weaken sufficiently by 2550 to end life on Earth (not the periodic weakening associated with magnetic poles shifting in the past) has led many to believe that the next organizing principle for civilization could be space migration— truly a long-range work/technology program.

2050 SCENARIO 2: POLITICAL/ECONOMIC TURMOIL—FUTURE DESPAIR

During the early 21st century, political leaders were so mired in short-term political conflicts and me-first, selfish economic thinking that they did not anticipate how fast artificial intelligence (AI), robotics, 3D/4D printing, synthetic biology, and other technologies would make business after business obsolete beginning dramatically in the late 2020s and early 2030s. Too many economists and lawyers who knew little of the coming technology-induced unemployment crowded out those with knowledge of what was coming. Corporate lobbyists protected short-term profit decisions. Most of the political/economic systems around the world did not reward long-term strategic planning but rewarded short-term profits and immediate political favors. Hence there were no long-term strategies in place to reduce the devastating impacts of the dramatic growth in unemployment around the world, especially in high- and middle-income countries.

The concentration of wealth continued during the first half of the 21st century as did the widening income gaps and employment-less economic growth. The return on investment in capital and technology continued to be far more than on labor, and the number of persons per services and products has dramatically fallen. Even though these problems were clear to all leaders as early as the mid-2010s, the political gridlock taking many forms (progressive vs. conservative; executive vs. legislative; augments vs. naturals; taxpayers vs. unemployed; Sunni vs. Shia; fundamentalist vs. liberal; urban vs. rural; debtor vs. creditor nations; scientists vs. populists; and rich vs. poor) around the world had become so bad that by the 2020s intelligent discourse about economic policy was dead.

Superficial news coverage and trivial social media so filled the public's attention that little time was spent to understand the gravity of technological changes. Even though capitalism, socialism, and communism were early industrial-age economic systems, any serious discussions of post-information-age economic systems were ignored.

Today's global workforce of 6 billion has only 1 billion employed, 1 billion self-employed, 2 billion in the informal economy, and 2 billion unemployed or in transition. About 3 billion people were employed in the early 21ˢᵗ century. Today there are only 2 billion, either employed by others or self-employed. Hence, new technologies over the last several decades did not create more new kinds of employment than they replaced. As a result, two thirds of the word's workforce is either in the informal economy or unemployed. Weakened economies and financial systems cannot support aging societies and massive youth unemployment. Since guaranteed income systems were not in place, social strife and the growth of cybercrimes, terrorism, corporate militias, and organized crime dominate much of world affairs.

Walking into the Future Technologically Blind

Localization of production via 3D/4D printing, robotics, and synthetic biology each improved by artificial intelligence dramatically reduced the need for international trade. The comparative advantage of low wage labor in Asia and Africa quickly evaporated during the late 2020s and the early 2030s. As a result, their export income began to fall, unemployment began to increase, and instability proliferated, especially in those areas with large youth populations. Aggregate demand was too low, slowing innovations, creating periodic recessions. Governments, even in the richer areas, are still lurching from one financial crisis to the next unable to meet full financial obligations in health care, retirement benefits, and infrastructure repairs. This forced governments to begin to do serious analysis and goal-setting more holistically and synergistically. They began to seriously assess the technologies of automation, such as artificial intelligence, robotics, synthetic biology, 3D/4D printing and bio-printing, IoT (Internet of Things), drones (and other autonomous vehicles), nanotechnology, VR (virtual reality) and AR (augmented reality), cloud analytics, and the extraordinary synergies among these technologies. All together these became known as Next Tech or NT. But strategies created by a set of political leaders were ignored by the next set of leaders, resulting in no strategic continuity and hence there was little progress in addressing these issues.

Stockholders wanted short-term ROI, which focused on technology cutting labor costs and making long-term investment less likely. Politicians ignored futurists and others with technologically sophisticated insights of what was coming. The gap between politics and knowledge grew beyond description. The world listened habitually to popularized ignorance and shunned knowledge. Anti-science movements began to proliferate.

Educational systems were unable to keep up with technological change, leaving too many without the ability to get a job or create their self-employment. Many excellent Internet-based global systems were and still are available, but not enough take advantage of these and some radical religious groups continue to block some educational material. Although our understanding of the brain and AI systems improved dramatically during the 2020s and 2030s, there was little focus on increasing intelligence, creativity, critical thinking, human relations, philosophy, ethics, and values. Instead, government education systems focused on out-of-date knowledge and social order.

Urban growth began to slow in the 2030s as many unemployed left the cities to take up rural high-tech subsistence agriculture and the use of 3D/4D and other advanced technological means to produce their food, shelter, clothing, and other essentials. It was a "back to basics" survivalist social movement and mindset living off the electric grid but still connected to the Internet to find international income opportunities. With the general economic slowdown, the unemployed purchased fewer goods and services, further slowing the global economy and technologic proliferation. Today in 2050 nearly 4 billion people are either unemployed or in the informal economy, with little hope of a better future for them and their children.

Tech Unemployment

The impact of many forms of intelligent robots working seven days a week, 24 hours a day, 365 days a year without the need for salaries, food, vacations, or medical and retirement benefits was much greater on unemployment than previously anticipated by the dominant political and media cultures. AI and robotic systems made far fewer errors and worked in conditions that required far more complexity than humans could handle and environmental conditions not tolerable by humans. As AI learned how to learn and robots developed reliable vision and voice recognition, the replacement of jobs began to accelerate. Some were smart enough to invest in what replaced them. For example, some truck drivers invested into driverless trucks and managed their contracts and routing from home.

Population growth in Africa and South Asia was faster than new jobs could be created by NT; leaving many in subsistence agriculture, while others migrated to richer countries. Some of the AIDS orphans in Africa, Eastern Europe, and Asia grew up to be hardened criminals making the cities more dangerous today.

As average worldwide unemployment rates passed 15–20% in the early 2020s, coalitions of labor unions, occupy protests, human rights movements, environmentalists, feminists, and other social networks began meeting in major cities around the world to demand jobs or some form of guaranteed income. Public works programs were created, but had little impact on the big picture of the technological unemployment of the 2030s. The sharing economies have helped prevent many from falling into despair, but quality control turned out to be nearly impossible to implement; thefts and violent crimes increased along with criminal computer hackers countering sharing companies' software controls. Hence, the sharing economy was prevented from becoming a dominant economic form. Nevertheless, there were some successes with on-line barter exchanges, 3D/4D community maker hubs, and alternative currencies for the unemployed. The empty, rusting factory covered in foliage has become the symbol of poor planning and little anticipation of the future.

Social Strife

As a result, there is a re-emergence of secret societies and crime families throughout the world in response to ineffective governance. As a generalization, where governments provide basic services there was more social stability; where governments were not able to predictably do this there was more social chaos. The failure of national governments and international organizations to make serious decisions has made them nearly irrelevant. As people began to take the law into their own hands, government crackdowns increased. Large corporations have hired legions of mercenaries to protect their businesses and many moved to small islands and ocean habitats (and other safer locations). Many believe large corporations are controlling the world today with greater influence than nation-states.

Social Darwinism seems to be a growing world "religion" leading to a very tough social fabric where conniving, cheating, physical violence, and deception characterizes much of human interactions. Vacuous power, not love or trust, is the social bonding force among many around the world.

Conventional arts and media focused on ways to keep the masses busy, while other arts and media decried government, crime, and the lack of global ethics. Neither focused on the need to change culture to anticipate and adapt to NT altering the culture of employment, work, and jobs.

To help restore civil order, many nations have welcomed martial law, the suspension of civil rights, and increased technological surveillance. The trends toward democratization in the late 20th century and early 21st century have clearly reversed today. However, with the weakened national governments, city governments have become more powerful today than in the early 21st century. Many international associations of city mayors have become more effective governance systems of doing the peoples' business. Although these too are penetrated by organized crime, they at least continue to manage urban infrastructures and police social protests and revolutionary movements.

Rumors of information warfare conducted among governments, corporations, terrorists, organized crime, and business marketing consultants have increased the sense of paranoia. No one is sure what or whom to believe or trust. Even robot naval ships seemed to have jammed each other's management of robot planes and robot submarines across the high seas, making it unclear who caused what. Governments may be reluctant to say much about these cyber-attacks, as they are not sure what responses to make and to whom.

Simultaneously, hedonism is on the rise, as people see little light at the end of the tunnel. Freely available 24/7 VR immersive social media ("cyber heroin") keeps people occupied, diverting attention from revolutionary movements. Social divides continue between working taxpayers and the unemployed on welfare. New social divisions are now increasing between the richer technologically augmented and the poorer "naturals."

From Artificial Narrow Intelligence (ANI) to Artificial General Intelligence (AGI) to Artificial Super Intelligence (ASI) and other Next Technologies (NT)

"We will all become augmented geniuses!" declared AGI visionaries, who spoke of the first worldwide renaissance or enlightenment, but they forgot that "all" included criminals, terrorists, and others who preyed upon the vulnerable. The AI arms race between good and evil has taken on horrific proportions. It seemed that no matter how well-intentioned the inventors of new technologies were, immoral geniuses would turn them against the good majority. Despair was growing.

As mentioned above, nanotechnology, synthetic biology, photonics, cognitive science, IoT, artificial intelligence, big data, block chain, drones, robotics, 3D and bio-printing, and augmented/virtual realities collectively became known as Next Tech or NT. Although NTs have increased human life span and intelligence and solved many problems in health and agriculture, the misuse of some have created many of the problems we face today.

By the mid to late 2020s the economies of scale brought the price of IoT glasses and smart clothing so low that many people were given these glasses and clothing free as part of employee benefits, insurance policies, marketing programs, and credit systems. This accelerated diffusion within poorer countries. UNICEF, the World Health Organization, UNESCO, and international development agencies also helped with distribution in poorer regions. Speech recognition and synthesis, integrated in nearly everything, made technology transfer far more successful than originally deemed possible by the UN Development Programme's Tele-volunteers, who did much to help the poorest regions understand and use the benefits from these new technologies. Google and Facebook helped to complete Internet access to the poorest regions of the world. As a result, many remote villages in the poorest countries have cyberspace access for tele-education, tele-work, tele-medicine, tele-commerce, and tele-nearly-anything. However, this also gave more people the ability to be far more destructive.

Global Regulation of NT

To better regulate NT, governments agreed to create the International S&T Organization (ISTO) as a software collective intelligence system to regulate by information power rather than by increasingly irrelevant international law. Governments could not keep up with technological change. This made their attempts at regulation irrelevant and drove controversial S&T research underground, resulting in products that were less safe and sold by criminal networks.

In reaction to several biotech accidents and drone traffic control AI disasters, a series of meetings were held with recognized eminent S&T experts. They decided how to control science and technology and limit access to developments that could be used by terrorists, criminals, and others in destructive ways. The participants were selected through the InterAcademy Partnership (composed of national academies of science, engineering, and medicine), the International Council of Scientific Unions, S&T interest groups, and private-sector R&D firms. The meetings created definitions, guidelines, intervention criteria, drafts for international treaties, and the charter for ISTO. Each time the eminent group reached a consensus on some element of the strategy, it was discussed around the world and a broader social consensus was created. This led to treaties and the establishment of some regulatory power of ISTO in concert with the UN Security Council.

The UN Security Council authorized intervention to terminate lines of scientific inquiry in genetic modification, nanoweapons, and the potential of runaway particle physics experiments. Several countries that proved to have insufficient security measures accepted UN Security Council–appointed advisors to improve the situation. Although the motivation for creating ISTO was good, unfortunately the online systems of ISTO became a new theater for information and cyber warfare that could not be trusted and hence became useless. It was very depressing that such a well-structured system failed to make the world a safer place.

Although software experts warned that AI should be equipped with off-switches, developers were so many, and developing new capabilities so fast, that few safeguards were put in place. Because there was little collaboration in creating good initial conditions for AGI, this potentially beneficial technology has become just another extension of the human condition with all its egotistical as well as benevolent behaviors. It was expected that AI would be controlled by humans setting AI's goals, but as Avatars were given AI in computer games, the line between artificial general and super intelligence began to blur as some AGI developed its own goals, leading to a few disasters that would finally be countered by coordinating government cyber AI units, corporate AI teams, and global A-HATs (ad hoc hack-a-thons that grew out of Anonymous). These cyber heroes are still collaborating today to head off future AGI disasters and are hopefully about to figure out how to manage relations with artificial super intelligence (ASI).

As artificial narrow intelligence (ANI) began rapidly creating its own ANI and in parallel AGI was developed in the 2030s, organized crime set up dummy corporations to recruit advanced computer game programmers to make financial games that were then adapted by others in organized crime to steal financial assets and fix election results, thus leading to the power of organized crime today. AI automatic trading systems have also been attacked by cyber criminals hired by those protected by a complex set of shell corporations.

The merger of virtual and augmented realities blurred the distinction with "real" reality in computer games, leading to accidental murders, paranoia, and deteriorating health conditions from cyber addiction or "cyber heroin."

Anti-Science and Neo-Luddite Movements

Many honorable people who otherwise would support advanced technology were so horrified by the abuse of technology that they joined anti-science and Neo-Luddite groups. The Neo-Luddite movement really took off when autonomous robot weapon systems massacred thousands of unemployed demonstrators simultaneously in New York, Mumbai, Tokyo, Kinshasa, Cairo, and Shanghai. Mobs burned robot factories and AI research facilities.

The ability to hack government and corporate systems was put together by a strange alliance of anarchists, terrorists, and organized crime. Subsequent cyber-attacks on the IoT, robot transportation, and health care systems have led to several Anti-Science and Neo-Luddite politicians taking over some major countries and nearly a third of UN organizations. The pro-science A-HATs and other cyber-art collectives have created computer games, popular music, and interactive VR systems to counter the Anti-Science movements. Unfortunately they seem locked in an unending intellectual arms race, only able to prevent things from getting even worse. Their recruiting message was "Never Again," referring to the "Son of Noah" – SON, a single individual who split off from the Neo-Luddites and created the synthetic biology attack that killed over 125 million people in 2035. Taking inspiration from the Bible, SON believed that the world had become so wicked it was time to start all over like the "Great Flood" thousands of years ago. Since then, other Neo-Luddite and religious terrorists have created and deployed dirty bombs, first used in the 2020s. These remain a current threat in major cities today, keeping martial law and police states in power and forcing A-HAT and government collaborations to reduce these threats.

Some business-university collaborations tried to skip the political know-nothings to chart a new course, but they were thwarted by ignorant government regulations, cynical media, and periodic urban riots of unemployed Neo-Luddites.

Geopolitical Turmoil

The periodic and ad hoc mergers of organized crime and terrorist separatists' sabotage have made the IoT a nightmare. When devices on the IoT malfunctioned or the occasional system collapses, people did not know if it was just a new software bug or sabotage and by whom or for what reason. This has increased a general sense of malaise and paranoia. The costs of insurance and security in all their forms continue to rise. To counter terrorism and organized crime, government cyber commands and business nanotech sensors connected in vast mesh networks and big data early warning systems have made privacy an illusion. Because governments were unable to create and implement a global strategy to counter organized crime, such crime now accounts for more than 15% of the world economy. Even governments' use of AI to predict and prevent crime is countered by the best hackers criminal money can buy. Organized crime buys and sells government and corporate decisions throughout the world on a daily basis like they used to buy and sell heroin.

Since nations are less cooperative, the UN Security Council and the UN Secretariat has become largely dysfunctional, providing instead a common source for government and corporate intelligence gathering and exchanges.

Wave after wave of migrations to the more stable European countries triggered nationalist political victories that nearly destroyed the EU. Global warming has created environmental migrations due to droughts, famines, and coastal sea water seeping into former freshwater agricultural lands. Changing ocean acidity, temperature, and currents have added to climate irregularity, loss of coral reefs, and release of ocean-trapped methane gas. Atmospheric CO_2 reached 700 ppm this year and climatologists now warn that if we reach 900–1000 ppm we will hit the tipping point of run-away greenhouse effect.

China's water/energy/food crises plus northwest secessionists, urban-rural and rich-poor divides, and increasing numbers of the unemployed have led to modern-day warlords filling the gap left by weakened central control. Cease-fire after cease-fire has broken down. Urban food riots and rural water wars increasingly fill the news.

Nanotech armies developed and sold by organized crime in the 2040s have changed the concept of political power and added to the world's political turmoil. Governments, corporations, and organize crime are engaged in a great intellectual arms race for global AI domination—half of all major military R&D budgets are now AI-related.

As a result of all this political turmoil, most of the UN Sustainable Development Goals were not achieved in 2030, and new goals for 2050 were not set due to political gridlocks and distrust of international institutions.

Humanity Uneasy about Artificial Super Intelligence (ASI) Prospects

The AGI that evolved beyond human control have become a new kind of intelligent species living in cyberspace. Anticipating this development, coalitions of governments, businesses, and academia created the United Cyber Command (UCC) to counter the threats of this new kind of species (or multi-species). However, no one is claiming success, and known UCC efforts have failed, leaving nothing safe. AI/robots create improved AI/robots without any control from humans.

Things started to happen that were not explainable other than that ASI was beginning to happen beyond our understanding. We had never faced a superior intelligence like this before. During pre-scientific times humanity created polytheistic gods to explain forces of nature they did not understand; today Techno-Animism is beginning to be a new kind of religion to explain the new anomalies that might be caused by ASI. Just as polytheists thousands of years ago believed that there were gods helping humans and gods punishing humans, so too many now believe there are many ASIs that ranged from good to bad for humanity. One wonders if pro-human ASI will ultimately fight anti-human ASI in a war we will never understand.

The gap between machine intelligence and what human's understand about what is happening is so wide many feel alienated and approach the future with despair. This post-Future Shock anomie seems to be increasing with no end in sight. There are rumors that some political, business, and AI leaders are quietly working to create a kind of hybrid AGI-TransInstitution as a new kind of governance system able to turn around the global situation. Even if true, no one really knows how this and ASI will relate.

2050 Scenario 3: If Humans Were Free—The Self-Actualization Economy

The transition to the Self-Actualization Economy has begun. Although this transition is not complete, we have come a long way. For the first time in history, humanity is engaged in a great conversation about what kind of civilization it wants and what we, as individuals and as a species, want to become. Movies, global cyber games, UN Summits, VR News, flash mob cyber teach-ins, and thought leaders probe the meaning of life and the possible future as never before. The historic shift from human labor and knowledge to machine labor and knowledge is clear: humanity is being freed from the necessity of having a job to earn a living and a job to achieve self-respect. This is initiating the transition from the job economy to the self-actualization economy.

Humanity began to break free from the anxiety and pressure to make a living when artificial narrow intelligence (ANI) became more universal and as artificial general intelligence (AGI) emerged in the mid-2030s, plus the basic income guarantee experiments in the early 21st century were shown to have positive effects in Brazil, Finland, Switzerland, and the Basque region of Spain. Earlier experiments on a smaller scale that gave basic income to groups in India, Liberia, Kenya, Namibia, and Uganda showed that the majority of people used the money more wisely than critics expected. People tended to use the income to make more income. These studies also showed that health increased, crime decreased, education improved, and self-employment increased contrary to the view that guaranteed income would make everyone lazy. Finland and the UK showed that their supplemental cash payment system that consolidated welfare programs was more efficient than complex bureaucracies.

As the world became increasingly aware in the 2020s that growth by itself was no longer increasing wages and employment, thought leaders began to call more loudly for new economic assumptions. Attempts to reduce the global unemployment situation such as changing tax credits, increasing the power of labor unions, improving STEM (science, technology, engineering, and mathematics) education, promoting job sharing, and reducing work hours helped but made only marginal differences. Something far more fundamental was happening. As the industrial revolution replaced muscles, so the AI revolution is replacing knowledgeable brains. As the numbers of unemployed continued to increase due to no fault of their own but due to new technologies, many began to lobby for a basic income for all. But the cost of living back then was still too high for national budgets to afford. It wasn't until the mid-2030s that the cost of living began to fall enough and government income began to increase enough that basic income systems became financially sustainable.

Today's 6 billion world workforce has 1 billion employed, 3 billion self-employed, 1 billion in the informal economy, and 1 billion in transition to self-employment. About 3 billion people were employed in the early 21st century. Today there are 4 billion, either employed by others or self-employed. Hence, new technology over the last several decades created as much or more new kinds of employment than it replaced. The concept of unemployment has lost its meaning to the new "Globals" generation.

Factors Reducing the Cost of Living

As artificial general intelligence began to integrate and manage countless artificial narrow intelligence (ANI) programs in the 2030s to maintain and improve the basic infrastructures of civilization from waste management and flood control of rivers to millions of robotic vehicles in the air, land, and sea, the cost of running cities and suburbs began to fall. AI/robotic urban people mover systems have made free public transportation possible in many cities.

Even some Hyperloop-connected cities have begun lowering their costs for high-speed transportation.

Advances in materials science, 3D/4D and bio-printing, biomimicry, nanotech graphene that lasts longer with less need for repairs, and other new technologies also brought down the costs of construction, fabrication, maintenance, water, energy, medical drugs, and retro-fitting infrastructures. Atomically precise manufacturing reduces costs by reducing pollution, friction, imperfections, and the material and energy costs per unit of production. Computational physics has found replacements for many scarce and expensive natural resources. Improved recycling and other green technologies have lowered costs of environmental maintenance. AI efficiency-managed transportation reduced operating costs, as has tele-commuting. Other energy costs have been reduced by low-energy nuclear reactions (LENRs), solar, wind, drilled hot rock geothermal, and massive storage systems.

More-efficient buildings that create their own energy have reduced the cost of shelter and environmental impacts. Most windows today come with imbedded nano-photovoltaic material. Even food costs have come down due to AI/robotic fresh- and saltwater agriculture, pure meat from genetics with growing animals, synthetic biology, and AI/robotic delivery systems from farm to mouth. Tele-health, tele-education, tele-everything has also lowered the cost of living. Since the universal basic income helps reduce stress, stress-related costs in health care and crime have also been reduced. AI and robots that are not paid can work 24 hours a day seven days per week, make far few errors, and receive no paid vacations or health or retirement benefits; the costs of insurance, production, maintenance, and labor were dramatically lowered.

Defense spending has been reduced since cyber systems are less expensive to maintain and build than industrial-age military systems. As the costs of many things continued to decrease, the budget requirements for universal basic income also decreased. This increased the belief that it would be possible to financially maintain universal payments to citizens.

MOOCs (Massive Open, Online Courses) and AI-augmented global education systems and apps have made it possible to offer free public education from early childhood to the PhD. Genomic personalized medicine with AI-augmented diagnostics, treatment, bio-printing, synthetic biology, and robotic surgery have also made it possible to offer public health care as a right of citizenship. Multi-material 3D/4D printers in community maker hubs continuously improved the quality of objects by rewriting software based on feedback from global sensor networks that evaluate the efficiency of previously printed objects around the world. Much software is free, able to be copied perfectly, instantly, and worldwide. The whole world is getting smarter together in real time. But there were still costs that had to be met and salaries to be paid.

New Income Sources for the Self-Actualization Economy

Although governments in the early 21st century were not sure whether new technologies would replace more jobs than they created, many leaders thought it wise to begin to seriously explore long-range financial strategies to address future large-scale unemployment. Studies were implemented to see if a guaranteed universal basic income could be financially sustainable to eliminate extreme poverty, reduce income gaps, and help the transition to new kinds of economies. In general these studies showed that around the mid-2030s the cost of living would fall and new income sources could be created to meet the costs of such universal income programs. Many came to believe that a handout to everyone was better than the social chaos of massive unemployment and poverty. Guaranteed basic income was seen as a social investment in parallel with technological, education, and defense investments. And the arguments that basic income would make the public lazy were put to rest by the experiments and research in many countries and cultures that showed this was not true.

Since the circumstances for each nation are different, the methods selected to pay for their citizens' basic income and make up for the loss of income taxes were also different. Averaged all together (for the countries reporting data) the new sources of income and their percent of contribution to the total of new costs for the basic income payments were:

20% from reduction of tax havens

12% from value-added tax (receipt with electronic signature at point of sale)

11% from carbon tax and other pollution taxes

11% from tax on massive wealth growth from new technologies

11% from license and tax robots

10% from leases and/or taxes from national resources

9% from Tobin tax on international financial transfers

9% from universal minimum corporate tax

7% from state-owned percentage of some corporations

The new AI system for international financial transfers was implemented as part of the global strategy to counter organized crime and corruption and in order to collect the Tobin tax. This had the additional benefit of dramatically eliminating tax havens, which provided new income to many governments. It was estimated that $18 trillion kept in tax havens was finally brought back into national economies. Some of the organized crime income trapped in the new international financial transfer system has also started flowing back to national treasuries.

Just as private cars used to be licensed and taxed, governments now tax robots, some forms of AI, and their creations. In the landmark U.S. Supreme Court ruling, when any AI is mature enough to demand its rights, it automatically gets them, including intellectual property rights over its creations. This also means it pays taxes on income it derives directly and from its creations.

Digitalization has dramatically reduced the marginal costs of production as has the global transition to renewable energy. The carbon taxes that used to raise significant revenue are nearly negligible now with the success of renewable energy, seawater agriculture, and growing pure meat without growing animals. However, the self-actualization economy with increased self-employment is now beginning to grow, producing more income taxes than previously expected.

As these economic conditions began to change, it became increasingly clear that it just wasn't ethical to throw millions of people out on the streets because a robot or AI took their jobs. Since so much material and intellectual wealth was being created by combinations of AI, robotics, synthetic biology, nanotechnology, drones, 3D/4D and bio-printing, big data analytics, etc., often referred to as "Next Technologies" or NT, many argued that surely there had to be a way to give some of that new income to those unemployed that NT replaced. As NT built the foundations of more secure civilizations, they also continued to replace human labor in the production of food, shelter, and clothing, along with transportation, construction, health care, and education.

Naturally, the richer oil-endowed countries like Norway and the Gulf States were among the first to fully implement universal basic income or "citizens' wage" for all their people. To prevent unwanted migration, they required three years residency prior to payments.

In the United States, Congress was unable to pass a 35% flat tax to fund a guaranteed income in 2025. Its population was about 345 million then. Those arguing against the bill pointed out that a payment of $20,000/year per person would cost about $6.7 trillion/year—about the same as the whole federal budget then, and far less income would be taxable with rising unemployment in the coming years. Those arguing for it pointed out that children could receive 25% of what the adults would be paid; hence a family of two adults and two children would get $50,000/year not $80,000. They also argued that welfare systems would be consolidated, its universal nature would eliminate social stigma, it would unleash human creativity beyond anything witnessed in history, and some requirement could be added for public service. It seemed immoral to require all to work to pay for their livelihood when only a minority's employment was needed for the well-being of society. Surely the financial risk was less dangerous than the social risk of millions in poverty roaming the streets.

But as the cost of living began to fall, Congress took up the matter again in the early 2030s and finally passed the Omnibus Income Bill with flat taxes on individuals and corporations, environmental damage, and NT growth. At the same time synthetic biology industries were growing, producing new employment and national wealth. This made the government income picture much better than previously forecast.

One of the greatest benefits of synthetic biology was the creation of microbes that eat the plaque in our brains. This has prevented a cascade of health problems among the elderly and added quality years to our life spans. This dramatically reduced their medical costs, kept their minds sharp, and increased their self-employment activities. Their AI/Avatars search the semantic web for the most wonderful self-fulfilling activities with income possibilities and present them each morning as an array of exciting experiences to fill the day. All these new conditions have created a true renaissance of creativity and a joy of life for the elderly. This has made the elderly a financial asset more than a liability. Now they contribute to the richness of life rather than being a cost to their children and grandchildren. This was important, since life expectancy is now nearly 100 years and longevity research continues to produce breakthroughs. All together these new sources of income helped to address the worry that there would not be enough aggregate demand to buy the innovations of NT.

The new economics and NT have lowered the cost of living enough that the basic individual income needs on average worldwide have been reduced to under $10,000/year. Without free services such as public medical care, urban transportation, energy, and education, this might not have been possible. Initially special arrangements had to be made for those with disabilities and other special needs, but as AI/robotic systems improved as costs were lowered, it was no longer a financial burden on the basic payment systems.

The percent of a country's GDP for basic income payments varied widely depending on population size, GDP, and official poverty lines. Richer countries with falling population like Japan and South Korea had an easier time meeting payments.

Since increasing numbers of people were augmenting their basic income payments with new income found by their AI/Avatars and AI Apps, some are choosing to donate their basic income payments to charities, invest into new business startups to address global challenges, or have the government temporarily stop their payments. The wealthier have done this for years. The distribution of abundance has become more of an economic focus than the distribution of scarcity.

Some Technological Factors

The Great Brain Race of the 2020s among the brain projects of the U.S., China, and the EU synergized with the AI Race among Google, IBM, Facebook, Baidu, SAP, and universities such as ETH Zürich and MIT Boston have created the synergies that have led to the many variations of brain augmentation with AI systems we take for granted today. Our photonic lenses injected into our eyes keep us in immersive internet virtual and augmented reality all the time connected with anything or anybody. As a result, taking IQ tests have become irrelevant since anyone with augment-eyes can see and get the right answers to all the questions.

As computational neurobiologists and engineers began to collaborate across national and corporate boundaries, they identified and applied the principles of brain functions to better treat mental illness, increase human intelligence, and build better computer and AI systems. It is now possible for most to augment their brains to become behavioral geniuses, in a similar way that people augmented their eyesight with eyeglasses. Anyone who wants can get intelligence augments, which are now seen as the only way to keep up with the knowledge explosions and AI advances. However, it does come with a potential loss of privacy since AI hacking programs are everywhere. Nevertheless, human-AI symbiosis is now a key element of learning from early childhood through university and continuous adult learning. Epigenetic applications to create more compassionate genetically influenced behavior are now coupled with genetic enhancements to prevent the development of unethical or criminal geniuses.

When people accepted that intelligence could be improved like eyesight, Ministries of Education added increasing intelligence as an objective of education. AI and learning theory experts teamed up to create businesses to sell individual intelligence augmentation apps known as AI/Brainware, in addition to their advances in STEM and self-employment learning modules. Individuals with their own collective intelligence systems and their personal algorithms are inventing their daily work lives. Global Learning XPRIZE awarded in 2020 has led to literacy and numeracy for nearly all children before the age of six today. By the age of ten, most children have used augmented genius systems—as we used to augment our vision with glasses to public standards. We have come to accept personal augmentation of intelligence. The global effort to upgrade STEM education during the 2020s has helped people understand the S&T-induced changes occurring, even though it did not create as much employment as expected in the 2030s. Humans could not learn as fast as the 2030s versions of AGI. As STEM became less relevant, the learning focus shifted more toward self-paced inquiry-based learning for self-actualization and self-employment. Learning shifted from mastering a profession to mastering combinations of skills.

However, as the public began to believe in the mid-2020s that AGI would be created, there was a general anxiety that artificial super intelligence (ASI) would follow so quickly after AGI that human systems would not be ready to address a new more intelligent non-human "species." As a result two groups gained prominent attention: one to stop all research on AGI and the other to prove that AGI could be created with ethics so that as ASI evolved, it would not be a threat to humanity. They expected ASI to become something like "The Force" in the movie *Star Wars*. It surrounds us and penetrates us. It binds our Conscious-Technology civilization together. Although the anti-AGI efforts failed, they did force AI developers to cooperate quickly to make the AGI able to generate ASI that works synergistically today with humanity. Yes, we are now dependent on ASI that we don't fully understand, but then we are also dependent on Nature for genetics, gravity, oxygen, temperature, and many other things that we don't fully understand either.

Children today find it hard to imagine a world without AI/robots, just as their parents find it hard to imagine a world without smart phones, and their grandparents find it hard to imagine a world without the Internet.

Along with the microorganisms that eat the plaque in our brains, synthetic biology has also created environmentally friendly chemicals, personalized medicines, crop fertilizers, and buildings that clean the air, absorb CO_2, and biodegrade when new construction is needed. Early Clustered Regularly Interspaced Short Palindromic Repeats (CRISPR) gene editing technology and the newer methods of today have nearly eliminated genetic-related disease, including most forms of mental illness.

The synergies among Moore's Law, ANI and AGI, and computational science accelerated our knowledge of the world and applications to dramatically improve the human condition. These synergies have created so much innovation that people joke about Synergs: One synerg is the production of one innovation per hour. This is the origin of the Global Synergs Awards for the most prolific inventions per year given in parallel to the Nobel Prizes for past achievements. Innovations multiplied as millions of people donated their unused computer capacity to solve problems. This coordination has created thousands of ad hoc super computers at virtually no cost.

The International Science and Technology Organization (ISTO) created the S&T collective intelligence system. It has become the "go to" place for students as well as top engineers and politicians to help make better S&T decisions. The sophistication of the interface is calibrated to each user's abilities and preferences. All could see the pros and cons of each NT advance, international standards, licensing, investments, and forecasts all updated in real time. The simultaneity of globally shared intelligence reduced the success of previous marketing spins, exploitation of the less knowledgeable, and manipulations by power elites. Small fees paid to ISTO for licensing agreements and other business deals recorded in block chains reached though ISTO's online systems provided financial sustainability and equal access for all.

ISTO serves as a form of international regulation by information power. Elon Musk's Future of Life Institute funded safe AI innovations that led to cooperation among many AI experts and Microsoft, Alibaba, Baidu, InfoSys, Google, and the UN's ISTO to create the initial conditions for safer ANI and AGI with real-time feedback interactions with humans that have helped create our conscious-technology age today. This has remained successful enough to avoid government and international regulations that would have been too slow to keep up with ANI and AGI advances.

The UN's Sustainable Development Goal to eliminate extreme poverty was essentially achieved by 2030. Closed-environment-smart agriculture, synthetic biology, seawater agriculture, electric robot cars, vertical urban farms, and pure meat without growing animals are feeding the world with a healthier, less expensive diet and with lower environmental impacts. Millions of robot vehicles fly the skies, sail the oceans, and drive on roads day and night controlled by AI systems around the world.

Nanotech sensors connected in mesh networks in public spaces have prevented much of the individual and group terrorism of the past. Advances in cognitive and behavior sciences have reduced the number of mentally ill from becoming terrorists and cyber criminals, as have the anxiety-reducing universal basic income. Cultural mergers of mystic attitudes toward life with technocratic knowledge of life have made more responsible and harmonious societies. Humanity is clearly maturing as a more ethical species, as evidenced by the success of ISO's (standards set by the International Organization for Standards) evolution to a global participatory ethics system.

Every four years the Olympic movement reinforced this maturing global consciousness through its games in both cyber and three-dimensional space. In 2040, when the Mars Pioneers won the first Olympic competition in solar sailing between Earth and lunar orbits, humanity seemed to pass some threshold of consciousness. We became aware that we were no longer an Earth-only species but will become a space-faring one. Nearly 2,500 people now work in space communities in orbit, on the moon, and on Mars, giving a new frontier for human imagination and advances in civilization.

The debates about the potential of extraterrestrial contact have forced us to think beyond our geographic and ethnic boundaries. Additionally, scientific breakthroughs, the increasing ease of international and near-space travel, and the constant global communications among people of different views on Earth and near-space have also helped broaden our individual and collective perspectives. As a result, people are replacing their more parochial views and consider global ethics more seriously. Not all people value love, truth, fairness, family, freedom, and belonging, but far more than in the 20th century and enough to keep a relatively peaceful world. Although ethnic prejudice still exists, it has been held in check more effectively than during the previous century.

Changing Nature of Work and Economic Culture

People used to worry about the risk of a jobless economic recovery, and now they welcome the increasing freedom that it brought. More and more people around the world are beginning to see the purpose of work is self-actualization in harmony with the social and natural enlightenments. Work becomes a pleasure, a method for self-actualization, and a way to create meaning for one's life. Since the various forms of guaranteed basic income reduced anxiety about basic financial needs, it freed people to explore what they think is their purpose in life.

As a result, the majority of humanity has the time to pursue causes that have helped build a better future, whether they have chosen a rural lifestyle living off-grid, or living at sea in floating or cruising communities, or living for the excitement of intense urban encounters. Since humanity has progressed at the expense of the environment, most believed it was now time to correct the negative environmental trends.

For example, environmental groups helped to discredit the concept of economic growth at any cost and created tremendous pressure on the U.S. and China to more seriously address climate change, since these countries were the biggest economies and polluters. Thanks to the U.S.-China joint goal to reduce CO_2 to 350 parts per million (ppm) and their R&D program that many nations, corporations, NGOs, and universities have joined, we now see a "whole-of-world" response to climate change. All agree that this R&D program is one of the best international agreements in history. Massive saltwater AI/robotic agriculture farms have been built along brown barren coastlines of the world. These have been financed in part by cap and trade programs because coastline seawater agriculture creates green growth areas absorbing CO_2. These coastal seawater farms produce shrimp and other foods as well as algae used for fuel, fertilizer, biopolymers, and even feedstock to grow meat without growing animals, which further reduces greenhouse gases per unit of nutrition. It also reduced pressure on freshwater agriculture while eliminating the problem with droughts—since seawater agriculture does not need rain. Micro-batteries charged by and attached to everything from buildings to our bodies have virtually eliminated the cost of personal energy.

Thousands of 100-mile-long robotically managed closed-environment agricultural tubes, interspersed with photovoltaic strips across the Sahel, produced much of the food for Africa and exports to Asia and Europe. Surplus energy from the photovoltaic strips is currently exported by wireless transmission to Earth orbit and relayed worldwide via satellite to terrestrial rectennas connected to local energy grids. Wind-induced pressurized water vapor jet systems have dramatically lowered the cost of desalination. And the internal combustion system for transportation has been replaced by electric and hydrogen systems.

The U.S.-China Goal is one of many stories of how the basic income guarantee freed people to pursue causes that have improved the human condition. It also changed the concept of status and inequality. The importance of the concept of inequality began to change around 2035-2045, since inequality assumes equal or unequal to some standard like income. As more people became self-sufficient, creating their own lives, they had their own individual standards of living well. Self-actualization is becoming more important as long as the basic necessities are covered by a basic income system. This also gives people more time to form or integrate into virtual communicates of mutual interest and expression. Being boring or bored is the new poverty; while working on something exciting to improve the world is the new cool, the new status, and the new wealth.

ANI systems have slowly but surely given way to a global tech commons of AGI to run global artificial brains without ownership—similar to how no one owns the Internet and Uber does not own taxies. Capitalism promotes private ownership; communism promotes state ownership; and the self-actualization economy promotes non-ownership, like the Internet. We still have private and state ownership today, but much of the creative growth is in non-ownership. This is also coupled with no or little restrictions to free usership. People did make money on their use of the NT means of production without owning these means of production. As the percent of people employed by corporations decreased and percent of self-employed increased, individual power began to increase relative to government and corporate power. This tended to increase the cultural acceptance of the self-actualization economy, as did self-organizing groups on the Internet.

People and companies are increasingly seeking qualitivity instead of productivity and synergy rather than competition. Business learning systems now teach synergetic intelligence, synergetic advantage, synergetic strategy, not just competitive intelligence, competitive advantage, and competitive strategy. Thought leaders around the world began discussing how to create synergies rather than only thinking in terms of trade-offs. Instead of fairness vs. return on investment, what synergies are possible to produce a good return on investment with fairness? The same with social values vs. market values or solidarity vs. efficiency. Inter-religious dialogues and ISO standards have contributed to these discussions of a more synergistic approach to life.

Increasing numbers of people have become part-time investors—not just in traditional stock markets but direct investments into individuals via crowd-sourced Kickstarter-like systems. Decentralization in its many forms, plus crowd funding, has helped reduce the concentration of wealth and income gaps. Human creativity is increasingly the norm as people stopped wasting time earning a living in jobs that stifled creativity. Since everybody can connect to nearly everybody and everything around the world, AI/Avatars using smart contracts make it easy to create new work and barter opportunities that are exciting and develop one's potential.

The "Invest in What Replaces You" movement was initiated by truck drivers who were able to buy into robot trucks and manage their schedules from online exchanges created by their labor union. These online exchanges had forecasts of how many years some jobs would remain, with recommendations of how much money should be earned each year to be able to invest in what replaces them. Since the hours of truck driving were far more than the hours managing the schedule of robot trucks, drivers had more time to explore new interests and more self-fulfilling work. While still employed, some people advertised their hobbies on Facebook and other forms of social media to begin to find markets for what they liked to do. This helped their transition to self-employment after their jobs were automated.

As societies became better educated, they were less interested in having bosses. Just as children require parents to be in charge but less so as they grow up, so too society at large is more interested in self-directed living. As society matures, personal AI/Avatars augment our intelligence guiding and assisting us throughout the day and finding interesting opportunities while we sleep.

AI engineers created new forms of notation and symbols that enabled the general public to understand the sophisticated world of 2050. These new forms made the global education systems more intelligible to a broad range of people. These notations and symbols are credited with helping transcultural collaboration. Many of the new kinds of perceptions of reality and ways of knowing were aided by using these new forms of notation.

The sharing economy pioneered by Uber and Airbnb in the early 21st century extends now to the sharing realities among people directly. It has created such a diversity of cultures that it is hard for anthropologists to keep up. The world of the mind and imagination dominates our daily lives with the integration of augmented reality, virtual reality, and AI systems, all accelerated by increasing numbers of people that use genius augmentations. The speed of feedback from inquiry to intelligent response is so fast today that curiosity has become a normal state of mind.

Some New Institutions for Old Problems

National economic TransInstitutions (composed of self-selected leaders in government, business, universities, NGOs, and others) held periodic national strategy workshops to review progress on their country's transition from the job economy to the self-actualization economy. Results of these annual national strategy audits were shared among nations to improve and implement strategic synergies. One of their first recommendations was to meet with filmmakers, music writers, entertainers, anthropologists, futurists, and philosophers to create images, scenarios, and concepts to make positive future visions and changes "more real." Memetic engineers worked with advertising companies to insert memes in ads to help the cultural transformation while selling products. The World Billionaires Club on strategic philanthropy helped to make all this happen. The stimulus for the Media/Arts Alliance's creating the "One Species" movement came from the first of these strategy workshops. The movement inspired the creation of movies, music, urban immersive environments, and the World Cyber Game that helped many to have the courage to explore their own value to society and become self-employed. Entrepreneurial spirit and stewardship have replaced the welfare attitude. The "AI/Augment" and "Invest in What Replaces You" campaigns were also furthered by the Media/Arts Alliance.

Several cyber TransInstitutions with AI/AGI augmentation continue to counter the growth of cyber-attacks, acting like complex adaptive systems that continually set new kinds of cyber traps and response systems. Information warfare is held in check by anticipatory collective intelligence systems that act as early warning systems to alert the public about manipulation of information flows. Many people freed to explore their own interests began to actively counter the terrorist and crime mindsets by being more active in community meetings, social media, NGO newsletters, talking with songwriters and religious leaders, and even using DNA kits to provide evidence to police.

The cybercriminal data havens in ocean floating platforms and ground cyber bunkers that managed cyber-attacks for organized crime and terrorists were countered both by AI software attacks and government commandos who physically invaded these locations. In some cases when governments moved too slowly, Anonymous and other Cyber-Partisans believed they had the right to take down the cyber bunkers by their own means.

Organized crime is finally shrinking due to the global strategy initiated by the IMF that established the Financial Prosecution System (FPS) in cooperation with the International Criminal Court (ICC) to complement national police and Interpol. In cooperation with these organizations, the FPS created a list of the largest organized crime leaders, prioritized by the amount of money each laundered. FPS worked down the list, prosecuting one mega criminal at a time. It prepared legal cases, identified suspects' assets that could be frozen or seized, established the current location of the suspects in cooperation with Interpol, assessed the local authorities' ability to make an arrest, and when all the conditions were ready, FPS would order the arrest, freeze the assets, and send the case to one of a number of preselected courts. These courts, like UN peacekeeping forces, were deputized and trained to be ready for instant duty. When investigations were complete, international arrest orders were executed to apprehend the criminal(s), simultaneously with orders to freeze access to their assets, open the court case, and then proceed to the next mega criminal leader on the priority list. Courts are selected outside the accused's countries. Although extradition is accepted by the UN Convention against Transnational Organized Crime, a new protocol was necessary for courts to be deputized by the ICC like military forces for UN peacekeeping. Each time a court was needed, it was selected via a lottery system among volunteering countries. After the initial government funding, the FPS became independent, receiving its financial support from frozen or seized assets of convicted criminals rather than depending on government contributions that could be subject to bribery by organized crime. Countries that made the arrests and courts that prosecuted the cases receive reimbursements from the frozen criminal assets.

ENDING COMMENTS....

By 2050 the world had finally achieved a global economy that appears to be environmentally sustainable while providing nearly all people with the basic necessities of life and the majority with a comfortable living. The resulting social stability has created a world in relative peace, exploring possible futures for the second half of the 21st century. Some believe that NT was the key to this relative success, others that the development of the human potential in the self-actualization economy was more fundamental, and still others that political and economic policies such as various forms of universal basic income made the difference. All three themes were important, synergizing, and mutually reinforcing.

The distinctions between human consciousness and AI in its many forms have become increasingly blurred or meaningless. Every possible Turing Test was passed years ago. Our interaction with AI is so complex and continuous that it rarely matters which is which. Even the distinctions among virtual reality, augmented reality, and physical reality are meaningless today. Civilization is becoming a continuum of consciousness and technology. We have added our reasoning, knowledge, and experience to AI augmented technology and the built environment. And at the same time we have integrated AI augmented technology in and on our bodies, making it unclear where our consciousness and technology begins and ends. Our Conscious-Technology Age opens a far more optimistic future than many in previous ages could have imagined. So today, the two key questions are: What kind of life are you creating? And are you boring or interesting?

WORKSHOPS TO EXPLORE LONG-RANGE STRATEGIES TO ADDRESS ISSUES IN THREE WORK/TECHNOLOGY 2050 GLOBAL SCENARIOS

Work/Tech 2050 workshops have been conducted in 17 countries, one for the Foresight European Network, and another 20 are in some stage of planning. Each workshop is a bit different, but in general they had five discussion groups:

1. Education and Learning
2. Government and Governance
3. Business and Labor
4. Science and Technology
5. Culture

The initial 100 suggestions that follow were drawn from the global scenarios and workshop reports. Suggestions that have a country in parentheses were made only by that country's workshop, while suggestions without country attribution were suggested by two or more workshops and/or were found in the scenarios.

Some suggestions not included in this summary were good ideas but not directed specifically at addressing long-range future work/technology issues or were obvious, such as *We need 'fresh' thinkers that dare to question the current system.*

Education and Learning
1. Make increasing intelligence an objective of education.
2. In parallel to STEM, create self-paced inquiry-based learning for self-actualization; retrain teachers as coaches using new AI tools with students.
3. Begin shift from mastering a profession to mastering skills.
4. Free Tele-education everywhere; ubiquitous, life-long learning systems.

5. Increased focus on developing creativity, critical thinking, human relations, philosophy, entrepreneurship (individual and teams), art, self-employment, social harmony, ethics, and values.

6. Know thyself to build and lead a meaningful working life with self-assessment of progress on one's own goals and objectives (Finland).

7. Intergenerational learning exchanges sharing competencies of elders with youth (Italy).

8. Consider experimental alternative education/learning models like Finland's education model that develops creativity, imagination, self-actualization.

9. Utilize robots and AI in education.

10. On-demand learning (also bite-sized) in learning portfolios (Germany).

11. Unify universities and vocational trainings (Italy).

12. Cooperation between schools and outside public good projects (Germany).

13. Focus on exponential technologies and team entrepreneurship (Italy).

14. Empathy training (Brazil).

15. Share the responsibility of parenting as an educational community (Mexico).

16. Create a global school for political leaders (Poland).

17. Teach technology while preserving thinking abilities (Israel).

18. Support hybrid education systems: STEM + social + economy.

19. Change curriculum at all levels to normalize self-employment (Spain).

20. Promote "communities of practice" (Brazil).

21. Transition from teaching centers to learning centers.

22. Benefit corporations to intervene in education systems (Italy).

23. Management of tech effects on students (Greece).

24. More future-oriented professional guidance (Greece).

25. 2030 education shifts more toward the humanities (Israel).

26. 2030-50 Private/public and machines/humans blurring make ethics the cultural theme (Italy).

27. Support Education X-Prize and other efforts to reach poorer regions of the world.

Government and Governance

1. Produce alternative cash flow projections for universal basic income (consider License/tax robots, AI and their creations, reduction of tax havens, value added tax, and taxes on carbon, massive wealth growth from new technologies, minimum corporate tax, etc.).

2. Include self-employment issues in political parties' agendas and manifestos to promote social dialog on these issues (Spain).

3. Training vouchers (Italy).

4. Work with other countries to establish the International S&T Organization.

5. 2050 Universal Basic Income introduced and financed by big companies and some governments (Israel).

6. Increase the role of international organizations in conflict resolution (Poland).

7. Establish law enforcing creation of sustainable businesses (Poland).

8. Decisionmaking based on collective intelligence (Brazil).

9. Create and implement a global counter organized crime strategy.

10. Add TransInstitutional law in addition to for-profit and non-profit law.

11. Training programs for politicians before governing and prototype governance methodologies (Brazil).

12. Tax on robotic work (Germany).

13. Easier participation for individuals in decisionmaking processes (South Korea).

14. Promote leisure, culture, tourism, and entertainment industries (South Korea).

15. E-Platform for citizens offering services (Greece).

16. By 2050 introduce a global system for resource sharing (Greece).

17. Enact policies for privacy concerns (South Korea).

18. Self-serving pension system with subsidies for those with lower income (Poland).

19. International coordination prior to implementing UBI would be wise to prevent enormous political and emigrational pressures that may arise with non-UBI countries (Israel).

20. The government, the employers across all industry sectors, and the labor unions should cooperate to create lifelong learning models (Israel).

Business and Labor

1. Invest in Kickstarter-like crowd sourcing to reduce the concentration of wealth.

2. Create personal AI/Avatars to support self-employment.

3. Create new labor unions to link one-person businesses to guarantee workers' rights in self-employment (South Korea).

4. Establish Labor/Business/Government Next Technologies Databases.

5. Develop individual augment genius apps.

6. International collaboration to create the International S&T Organization.

7. Conduct synergetic intelligence/advantage/strategy, as well as competitive intelligence/advantage/strategy, and teach synergy in business schools.

8. Labor unions focus more on maintaining income than keeping specific jobs and initiate Augment Movement to invest in tech to augment rather than replace labor.

9. Popularization of social capital and corporate shared value (Poland).

10. Foster one-person businesses, micro finance, and business training.

11. Develop ways to measure "Qualitivity" as well as "Productivity."

12. Memes in advertisements to help create the cultural transition.

13. Create category for Benefit Corporations.

14. World Billionaires Club on Global Strategic Philanthropy to address income gap.

15. World Cyber Game to explore self-employment and Self-Actualization Economy.
16. Promote circular economy as well as self-actualization economy.
17. Build resilience of workers for the hybridity of work, mixed income with UBI.
18. Develop ways for companies and employees to create ethical, aesthetic, and social value besides economic and material value.
19. Shorter work hours, job-sharing, and work-at-home (Germany).
20. Use block chain and cripto currencies to invent alternative economies.
21. Encourage business that produce experiences instead of physical products (Brazil).
22. Focus more on exporting knowledge than physical products (Netherlands).
23. Special Awards for companies that pay the most taxes (South Korea).
24. Create platforms to discuss future of employment (Spain).
25. Create an observatory of employment and technology trends (Spain).
26. Change trade unions' attitudes toward an attitude that helps to build the relationships of future businesses (Spain).
27. Recognize the basic income as an universal right (Spain).
28. Increase integration of government/business/people (Italy).
29. Develop profit opportunities for caring economies (Spain).
30. Businesses focus on making people happy, not just creating profits (South Korea).
31. Encourage work from home (Mexico).

Science and Technology
1. Augment Movement: Tech to augment humans, not replace them.
2. Identify likely impacts of Narrow AI vs. General AI, by years.
3. Forecast how synthetic biology might create more jobs than AI replaces.
4. Forecast synergies among the full range of new tech—NTs.

5. Create national policies/standards for IoT (Brazil).
6. Establish International S&T Organization as an online collective intelligence system not as a new bureaucracy.
7. Promote public participation, and even participation of the consumers, in the ownership of patents (Spain).
8. Internet for all with malicious usage prevention (Poland).
9. Use AI to search for and create jobs and match them to people (USA).
10. Invest in predictive/preventative health systems (Brazil).
11. Biotech for in-house food production via bio-gene-sciences (Italy).
12. Implement schemes to promote and support work from home.
13. Solar energy, autonomous transporters to free individuals (Italy).
14. Develop ultra-fast transport systems like the Hyperloop (Poland).
15. By 2030 create World Integrated Energy Corp to create enough wealth to invest in space exploration enhanced by AI (South Korea).
16. Create online platforms for participatory democracy (Brazil).
17. Socialize tech, R&D for social concerns (Spain).
18. Science focused on exploration (Poland).
19. Nearly 100% renewable energy by 2050 goal with stable base load (Poland).
20. Automate production/services to free creative development (Poland).

Culture
1. Explore cultural transition to self-actualization economy via the arts, media, entertainment, celebrities, and computer games.
2. Media/Arts Alliance to create and help new social movements:
   a. Self-Employment as new norm
   b. One Species
   c. Tech to augment human capacity, not replace humans
   d. Self-Actualization Economy
   e. Invest in what replaces you

     f.   Desire to work is human nature but change attitudes toward welfare and basic income (South Korea)

     g. Eco-empathy (Poland)

     h. Increasing focus on experience rather than things (Brazil)

     i.   Add more good news in media about positive actions (Brazil)

3. New social contract between the government and the governed:

     a. Universal basic income

     b. Security (lone-wolf terrorist more power in the future requires more public involvement)

4. Social campaign to understand S&T in development (Poland).

5. Move toward more civic, collaborative culture with reciprocity (Spain).

6. Create a Department of Collaboration in the Basque Government (Spain).

7. Valuing new experiences over accumulation of things (Brazil).

8. Invent ways to reduce social isolation of tele-workers (Poland).

5.
CONCLUSIONS

As a result of all the changes identified throughout this report, and others not yet on the horizon, far more individuals will have far more access to far more powerful capacities worldwide at far lower costs with far less control by power elites than in the past.

The 2017 State of the Future Index shows that we are winning more than losing, so we have no right to be pessimistic; however, where we are losing is very serious, so we cannot fall asleep either. After updating global developments and trends within the 15 Global Challenges for over 20 years, it is clear that humanity has the means to avoid potential disasters described in this report and to build a great future. Pessimism is an intellectually cowardly position that need not prove anything and can stunt the growth of innovative idealistic minds. Yet idealism untested by pessimism or unaware of the depth and magnitude of global problems fosters naiveté that can waste our time—and time is not on our side.

We need hard-headed pragmatic idealists willing to understand the depths of human depravity and heights of human wisdom. We need serious, coherent, and integrated understandings of mega-problems and mega-opportunities to identify and implement strategies on the scale necessary to address global challenges.

Doing everything right to address climate change or counter organized crime in one country will not make enough of a difference if others do not act as well. The challenges we face are transnational in scope and trans-institutional in solution. We need coordinated transnational implementation. Government and corporate future strategy units are proliferating, but they have yet to sufficiently influence decisions on the scale and speed necessary to address the complex, integrated, and global nature of accelerating change. Intergovernmental organizations and public-private collaborations are also increasing, but they too have to become far more effective. Humanity needs a global, multifaceted, general long-term view of the future with bold long-range goals to excite the imagination and inspire international collaboration.

Slowly but surely, a globally oriented planetary stewardship consciousness is emerging. Yet it may be too tolerant of the momentum of slow decisionmaking and glacial pace of cultural changes to improve our prospects. "Business as usual" future projections for water, food, unemployment, terrorism, organized crime, and environmental and information pollution lead to a series of complex human disasters. The stakes are too high to tolerate business as usual. The world is in a race between implementing ever-increasing ways to improve the human condition and the seemingly ever-increasing complexity and scale of global problems.

Since all of the 15 Global Challenges have to be addressed, strategies that can address multiple challenges should be emphasized. Figure 5.1 is an initial example of an overview of an integrated global strategy. Each element of it is a high-impact strategy in that it addresses multiple challenges. Improvements on this integrated strategy are welcome and will be used to update and improve it in GFIS. The world agreement on the UN Sustainable Development Goals is great step forward, and the integrated global strategies can help build political coherence to achieve that and address additional challenges as well.

Figure 5.1 Initial Draft Concept for Discussion of an Integrated Global Strategy

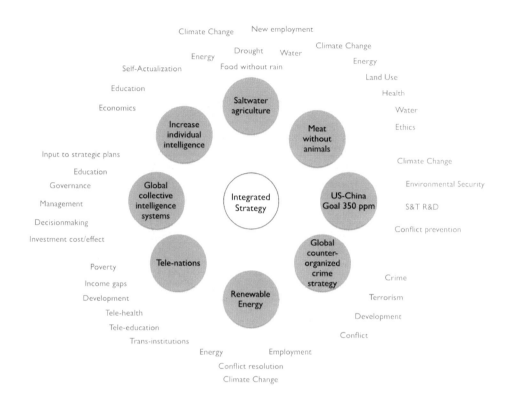

We should care about the whole world because the whole world will affect us—from new forms of terrorism and artificial intelligence to climate change and financial ethics. The *State of the Future 19.0* is offered to help us better understand the whole world of potential changes. Greater details are available and continuously updated online in the Global Futures Intelligence System. Your feedback and suggestions for improvement are always welcome at info@millennium-project.org.

APPENDICES

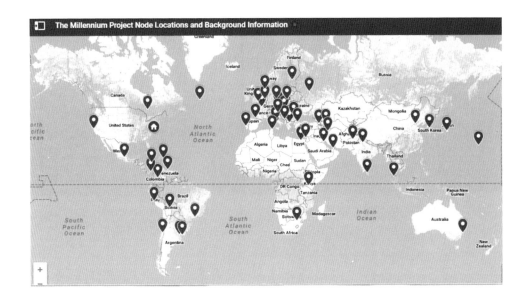

The Millennium Project Node Locations and Background Information

THE MILLENNIUM PROJECT GOVERNANCE

The Millennium Project Board of Directors
Amb. John W. McDonald, Chair
Concepción Olavarrieta, Vice Chair
Jerome Glenn, Executive Director
Charles Perrottet, Secretary
Elizabeth Florescu, Treasurer
Theodore Gordon, Member
Youngsook Park, Member
Cristina Puentez-Markides, Member

Ex Officio
José Cordeiro, RIBER (Ibero-America)
Cornelia Daheim, Foresight Europe Network

The Millennium Project Planning Committee
This committee gives guidance, works to insure objectivity and integration of a broad range of views, cultures, and diverse expertise. It is composed of all the Node Chairs and Co-Chairs listed in this appendix plus additional Futurists: Clem Bezold, Francisco Dallmeier, Hazel Henderson, Riel Miller, Charles Perrottet, Cristina Puentes-Markides, David Rejeski, Stanley G. Rosen, Paul Saffo, and Paul Werbos.

The Millennium Project Node Chairs and Co-Chairs

Argentina
Miguel Angel Gutierrez
Latin American Center for
Globalization & Prospective
Buenos Aires, Argentina

Australia
Anita Kelleher
Designer Futures
Inglewood, Australia

Azerbaijan
Reyhan Huseynova
Azerbaijan Future Studies Society
Baku, Azerbaijan

Bolivia
R. Verónica A. Agreda de Pazos
Rectora - Chancellor
Universidad Franz Tamayo -
UNIFRANZ
La Paz & Santa Cruz, Bolivia

Brazil
Arnoldo José de Hoyos
São Paulo Catholic University

Rosa Alegria
Perspektiva Consulting
São Paulo, Brazil

Jano Moreira de Souza
Future Lab
Universidade Federal do Rio de
Janeiro, Rio Janeiro, Brazil

Brussels-Area
Philippe Destatte
The Destree Institute
Namur, Belgium

Bulgaria
Mariana Todorova
Bulgarian Academy of Sciences

Boyan Ivantchev
Advance Equity and School for
Finance and Insurance
Sofia, Bulgaria

Canada
Karl Schroeder
Idea Couture
Toronto, ON, Canada

Caribbean
Yarima Sosa, FUNGLODE,
Santo Domingo

Beatriz Bechara de Borge
Observatorio del Caribe
Colombiano
Cartagena, Colombia

Central Europe
Pavel Novacek
Prague, Bratislava, and Warsaw

Chile
Luis Lira
Especialista en Desarrollo y
Planificación Territorial
Santiago, Chile

China
Zhouying Jin
Chinese Academy of Social
Sciences
Beijing, China

Colombia
Francisco José Mojica
Universidad Externado
Bogotá, Colombia

Croatia
Zoran Aralica and Diana Šimić
Croatian Institute for Future
Studies
Zagreb, Croatia

Czech Republic
Pavel Novacek
Palacky University
Olomouc, Czech Republic

Dominican Republic
Yarima Sosa
FUNGLODE
Santo Domingo, Dominican Rep.

East Africa
Arthur Muliro
Society for International
Development
Dar es Salaam, Kampala, Nairobi

Egypt
Kamal Zaki Mahmoud Shaeer
Egyptian-Arab Futures Research Ass.
Cairo, Egypt

Finland
(rotating Chairmanship)
Toni Ahlqvist, University of Oulu
Sirkka Heinonen, Finland Futures
Research Centre (FFRC)
Juha Kaskinen FFRC
Osmo Kuusi FFRC
Sari Söderlund FFRC
Finland

France
Saphia Richou
Prospective-Foresight Network
Paris, France

Georgia
Tamar Chachibaia
Georgian National
NanoInnovation Center
Tbilisi, Georgia

Germany
Cornelia Daheim
Future Impacts Consulting
Cologne, Germany

Greece
Stavros Mantzanakis
Emetris SA

Cristofilopoulos Epaminondas
Phemonoe Lab/Emetris, SA
Thessaloniki, Greece

Gulf Region
Ismail Al-Shatti
Gulf Inst. for Futures and
Strategic Studies

Ali Ameen
Kuwait Oil Company
Kuwait City, Kuwait

Hungary
Erzsébet Nováky
Corvinus University of Budapest

Mihály Simai
Hungarian Academy of Sciences
Budapest, Hungary

India
Mohan K. Tikku
Futurist/Journalist
New Delhi, India

Sudhir Desai
Srishti Institute
Bangalore, India

Iran
Mohsen Bahrami
Iranian Space Organization
Ministry of Communication and
Information Technology, and
Amirkabir Univ. of Technology
Tehran, Iran

Israel
Yair Sharan
The EPI/FIRST
Jerusalem, Israel

Aharon Hauptman
Tel Aviv University
Tel Aviv, Israel

Italy
Mara DiBerardo
J&J Production Company
Teramo Area, Italy

Simone Di Zio
Università G. d'Annunzio
Pescara, Italy

Japan
Sungjoo Ogino
Chiba, Japan

Shinji Matsumoto
CSP Corporation
Tokyo, Japan

Kenya
Arthur Muliro
Society for International
Development
Nairobi, Kenya

Republic of Korea
Youngsook Park
UN Future Forum
Seoul, Republic of Korea

Malaysia
Carol Wong
Genovasi
Office of the Prime Minister
Kuala Lumpur, Malaysia

Syed Isa Syed Alwi Al Hindwan
Algaetech International
Kuala Lumpur, Malaysia

Mexico
Concepción Olavarrieta
Nodo Mexicano. El Proyecto del
Milenio, A.C.
Mexico City, Mexico

Montenegro
Milan Maric
S&T Montenegro
Podgorica, Montenegro

Sanja Vlahovic
Ambassador to Italy

The Netherlands
Erica Bol
Conscious Future Design/
360 Foresight
Breda, The Netherlands

Pakistan
Puruesh Chaudhary
AGAHI and Foresight Lab
Islamabad, Pakistan

Shahid Mahmud
Interactive Group and Foresight Lab
Islamabad, Pakistan

Panama
Gabino Ayarza Sanchez
City of Knowledge Foundation
Clayton, Ancon
Panama City, Panama

Peru
Fernando Ortega
Peruvian Association of
Prospective and Future Studies
Lima, Peru

Poland
Norbert Kolos and Piotr
Jutkiewicz
4CF – Strategic Foresight
Warsaw, Poland

Romania
Adrian Pop
Centre for Regional and Global
Studies
Romanian Scientific Society for
Interdisciplinary Research
Bucharest, Romania

Russia
Nadezhda Gaponenko
The Institute for the Study of
Science of the Russian Academy
of Sciences
Moscow, Russia

South Africa
Rasigan Maharajh
Tshwane Univ. of Technology
Tshwane, South Africa

Southeast Europe
Blaz Golob
Belgrade, Ljubljana, Podgorica,
Zagreb

Spain
Ibon Zugasti
PROSPEKTIKER, S.A.
Donostia-San Sebastian, Spain

Silicon Valley
Brock Hinzmann
Futurist Consultant
Palo Alto, CA, USA

John J. Gottsman
Clarity Group
San Francisco, CA, USA

Slovakia
Ivan Klinec
Academy of Science
Bratislava, Slovakia

Slovenia
Blaz Golob
SmartIScity Ltd.
Ljubljana, Slovenia

Tanzania
Ali Hersi
Society for Internat. Development
Dar es Salaam, Tanzania

Tunisia
Jelel Ezzine
President, Tunisian Association
for the Advancement of Science,
Technology, and Innovation

Tunis, Tunisia.
Omar Zouaghi
Director, Ministry of Local Affairs
and the Environment
Tunis, Tunisia.

Turkey
Eray Yuksek
Turkish Futurists Association
Istanbul, Turkey

Uganda
Arthur Muliro
Society for International
Development
Kampala, Uganda

United Arab Emirates
Hind Almualla
Knowledge and Human
Development Authority
Dubai, UAE

Paul Epping
Philips Healthtech, MET
Chapter lead Dubai, Singularity Univ.
Dubai, UAE

United Kingdom
Rohit Talwar
Fast Future Research
London, England, UK

Uruguay
Lydia Garrido
Facultad Latinoamericana de
Ciencias Sociales – FLACSO
Montevideo, Uruguay

Venezuela
José Cordeiro
Red Iberoamericana de
Prospectiva, RIBER
Caracas, Venezuela

Arts/Media-Node
Kate McCallum
c3: Center for Conscious
Creativity
Los Angeles, CA, USA

Experimental Cyber-Node
In transition

CURRENT AND PREVIOUS SPONSORS

AGAHI, Islamabad, Pakistan (2016-17)

Academy of Scientific Research and Technology, Egypt (2013-2015)

Alan F. Kay & Hazel Henderson Foundation for Social Innovation,
    St. Augustine, FL (1996-2000)

Amana Institute, São Paulo, Brazil (2004)

Applied Materials, Santa Clara, California (2002–09)

Army Environmental Policy Institute, Arlington, Virginia (1996–2011)

Azerbaijan State Economic University (2009–2016)

Center for Strategic Studies under the President of Azerbaijan (2013)

City of Gimcheon (via UN Future Forum, South Korea) (2009–10)

Deloitte & Touche LLP, Cleveland, Ohio (1998–09)

The Diwan of His Highness the Amir of Kuwait (2010–11)

Environmental Law Institute, Washington, D.C. (2017)

Ford Motor Company, Dearborn, Michigan (1996–97, 2005–06)

Foundation for the Future, Bellevue, Washington (1997–98, 1999–2000, 2007–08)

General Motors, Warren, Michigan (1998–2003)

Government of the Republic of Korea (via UN Future Forum) (2007–08)

The Hershey Company, Hershey, Pennsylvania (2008–09)

Hughes Space and Communications, Los Angeles, California (1997–98, 2000)

Kuwait Oil Company (via Dar Almashora for Consulting) (2003–04)

Kuwait Petroleum Corporation (via Dar Almashora for Consulting) (2005–06)

Ministry of Communications, Republic of Azerbaijan (2007–11)

Ministry of Culture and Tourism, Azerbaijan (2013)

Ministry of Education and Presidential Commission on Education,
    Republic of Korea (2007)

Ministry of Education, Azerbaijan (2013)

Monsanto Company, St. Louis, Missouri (1996–98)

Motorola Corporation, Schaumburg, Illinois (1997)

NATO Science for Peace and Security Programme, Brussels, Belgium (2016-17)

Pioneer Hi-Bred International, West Des Moines, Iowa (1997)

Rockefeller Foundation, New York, N.Y. (2008–13)

Shell International (Royal Dutch Shell Petroleum Company), London, U.K. (1997)

UNESCO, Paris, France (1995, 2008–10)

United Nations Development Programme, New York, (1993–94)

United Nations University, Tokyo, Japan (1992–95, 1999–2000)

U.S. Department of Energy, Washington, D.C. (2000–03)

U.S. Environmental Protection Agency, Washington, D.C. (1992–93, 1996–97)

Universiti Sains Malaysia, Penang, Malaysia (2011)

Woodrow Wilson International Center for Scholars (Foresight & Governance Project), Washington, D.C. (2002)

World Bank (via World Perspectives, Inc., 2008; and GEF, 2012)

In-kind Support:

4CF – Strategic Foresight

EGADE (Business School), Tecnologico de Monterrey

George Washington University

Google

Harvard University

Smithsonian Institution

UNESCO

LIST OF FIGURES, TABLES, AND BOXES

State of the Future Index

Emerging Technologies for Potential Pre-detection of Terrorists and New Counter-Terrorism Strategies

Conclusions

ACRONYMS AND ABBREVIATIONS

AGI	artificial general intelligence
AI	artificial intelligence
AIDS	acquired immunodeficiency syndrome
ANI	artificial narrow intelligence
AR	augmented reality
ASI	artificial super intelligence
BIG	Basic Income Guaranty
BoP	Balance of Payments
CBRN	chemical, biological, radiological and nuclear
CDC	Centers for Disease Control and Prevention (U.S)
CEDAW	Convention on the Elimination of All Forms of Discrimination Against Women
CPIA	Corruption Perception Index (transparency, accountability, and corruption in the public sector)
CRISPR	Clustered Regularly Interspaced Short Palindromic Repeats
FAO	Food and Agriculture Organization
FPS	Financial Prosecution System
GDP	gross domestic product
gha	global hectare
GHG	greenhouse gas
GFIS	Global Futures Intelligence System
GNI	gross national income
GW	gigawatts
GWR	Great World Recession
HIV	human immunodeficiency virus
IAEA	International Atomic Energy Agency
ICBM	intercontinental ballistic missile
ICC	International Criminal Court
IMF	International Monetary Fund
IoT	Internet of Things

ISO	International Organization for Standardization
ISTO	International S&T Organization
kg	kilogram
kt	kiloton
LENR	low-energy nuclear reaction
MENA	Middle East and North Africa
MOOC	Massive Open, Online Course
NASA	National Aeronautics and Space Administration (U.S.)
NATO	North Atlantic Treaty Organization
NEP	New Economic Paradigm
NGO	nongovernmental organization
NIH	National Institutes of Health (U.S.)
NT	Next Tech
OECD	Organisation for Economic Co-operation and Development
OGP	Open Government Partnership
ppm	parts per million
PPP	purchasing power parity
R&D	research and development
RTD	Real-Time Delphi
S&T	science and technology
SDG	Sustainable Development Goal
SOFI	State of the Future Index
STEM	science, technology, engineering, and mathematics
TOC	transnational organized crime
UAE	United Arab Emirates
UBI	universal basic income
UCC	United Cyber Command
UNESCO	United Nations Educational, Scientific and Cultural Organization
UNHCR	United Nations High Commissioner on Refugees
VR	virtual reality
WHO	World Health Organization
WIPO	World Intellectual Property Organization

OTHER MILLENNIUM PROJECT RESEARCH AND PUBLICATIONS

The Global Futures Intelligence System (GFIS)

The Millennium Project has integrated all of its information, groups, and software into a "Global Futures Intelligence System". This gives users a new way to participate in The Millennium Project and to have access to all of our resources in one place. Subscribers can interact with all the elements of the system, make suggestions, initiate discussions with experts around the world, and search through a wealth of futures research (equivalent to over 10,000 pages) and access 39 futures research methods (equivalent to over 1,300 pages).

The material published in the *State of the Future* is being updated in GFIS on a continual basis with new data and details. The same is true with *Futures Research Methodology*. Some Real-Time Delphi studies and other research are also being made available as soon as they are completed.

The GFIS is not just new software, vast information, and global experts; it is also a system to produce synergies among these three elements for greater intelligence than their separate values. It is rather a global intelligence utility that provides decision makers, advisors, and educators with insights that reflect the consensus and/or range of views on the important issues of our time.

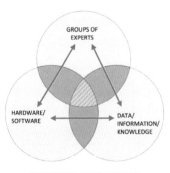

COLLECTIVE INTELLIGENCE

For more details and subscription see:
http://www.themp.org

Other Publications by The Millennium Project

Millennium Project reports provide a context for global thinking and potential for improved understanding of how humanity could work together for the best possible future. More detailed information on The Millennium Project publications is available on the Project's web site www.millennium-project.org.

Futures Research Methodology—V 3.0

The largest, most comprehensive collection of internationally peer-reviewed handbook on methods and tools to explore future possibilities ever assembled in one resource.

Over half of the chapters were written by the inventor of the method or by a significant contributor to the method's evolution.

It contains 39 chapters totaling about 1,300 pages.

Price: $49.50 US dollars
electronic download or CD

FUTUROS—Foresight Encyclopedic Dictionary

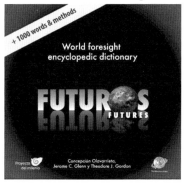

FUTURES is the most comprehensive futures studies encyclopedic dictionary that exists to date. It comprises over 1,000 terms and methods used in futures studies.

The work was initiated and coordinated by Concepción Olavarrieta, with review and edits by Theodore Gordon and Jerome Glenn, and with the contribution of more than 500 futurists from The Millennium Project network. It is available in English and Spanish.

Price: $50 US dollars
electronic download or CD

Previous *State of the Future* reports were translated into Arabic, Chinese, English, French, Korean, Persian, Romanian, and Spanish.